The Creation Guild

*Imagine the powerful flow that begins when
you build space to purposefully create*

by Janice Gallant

 FriesenPress

Suite 300 - 990 Fort St
Victoria, BC, V8V 3K2
Canada

www.friesenpress.com

ISBN
978-1-5255-0205-7 (Hardcover)
978-1-5255-0206-4 (Paperback)
978-1-5255-0207-1 (eBook)

1. BODY, MIND & SPIRIT

Distributed to the trade by The Ingram Book Company

Guild *(noun)*
- A medieval association of craftsmen or merchants, often having considerable power.
- An association of people for mutual aid or the pursuit of a common goal.
- The pursuit of the craft.

Synonyms: association, society, union, league organization, company, fellowship, club, lodge, brotherhood, fraternity, sisterhood, sorority.

The Creation Guild
- A group of people in pursuit of refining the craft of conscious manifestation
- A term I made up

Creative energy source has many names:
Source, Soul, God, Life Force, Higher Self, Light, Inner Being, God-Source, Spirit, In-Spirit, Higher Energy, Creative Source Energy, Divine Source, Creator, All There Is, Goddess, The Great Spirit, Allah, and many more.

Dedication:

To my husband John:
your love made me stronger, more confident,
and gave me the space to connect with my creative energy source.
Your strength, loyalty, and encouragement
has allowed me to be more loving, independent, and grateful.
You are forever my soulmate!
To our children Chayse, Shaine, and Emerald:
You are all amazing. This journey began for you.

From the bottom of my heart thank you for all the love, lessons
and fullness you have brought to my life!

Love you all forever!

Table of Contents

Introduction to
The Creation Guild

Every day a greater number of people are recognizing there is much more to creating our life than just floating down the river, hoping opportunities and luck will be on our individual journey. As awareness begins to emerge to a new level, there is increased need for guidance, from those further on the path, to help others build the life of their dreams.

Life does not have to be a struggle, and you can have the life you desire. We are all creators, working on great masterpieces in our lives. Whatever it is for each of us — career goals, fitness/health goals, artistic or musical creations, a new car, the love of your life — *whatever* you aspire to, having an open flow with your creative energy source heralds inspired and genius work. In this place, you will find a great power available to everyone, and when we consciously align and work with this flow, we discover many subtle nuances that can either block or enhance this available power. Tapping into the continuous flow of your creative energy source allows you to become the wholly aware architect who builds foundations for the full, rich beauty of your masterpieces to emerge.

Perhaps you have already felt this inspiration and power move through your life. Then you already know how elusive it can feel. It appears suddenly one day, and you feel like you are on top of the world, glowing with excitement and anticipation, only to find it dissipates without warning, leaving you in stagnant holes, feeling doubt or weakness or perhaps even monotony or boredom with your life. You may feel frustrated because it comes and goes so unpredictably. Learning from those of us who have been working with this energy for many years can save you frustration and help you grow more quickly than if left fumbling through this alone. It is time for everyone to align with this energy.

What exactly is this surge of power, and how can you continuously bask in it? What is the connection of this flow to the creations or manifestations in your life? *The Creation Guild* walks you through the basic steps of intentionally connecting with your creative energy source, feeling it, and using it to inspire your creations and build a life of your dreams. You will learn how to develop your awareness of all the essential tiny tweaks that refine and enhance your connection, tapping deeper into this powerful creative energy source.

There is no degree or paper that certifies someone as an expert in this field. You simply need to observe their life and their level of happiness to know if they have the expertise you can learn from. I have learned to quiet my mind, ask the right questions, and then listen. Through silence and observations, the learning came to me, but it took many years of working it out to understand how delicate this energy can be, and I learned the fine distinctions for creating.

It is not difficult, in fact, the steps are fairly simple. However, you need to be a dedicated learner, and it is immensely easier with some coaching from someone who has persevered through it. As a professional teacher, I present the steps in easy language to reveal these subtle energetic layers and set you on your way to having a clear and instantly accessible connection with your creative energy source. I teach you what to do each day and how to become finely tuned to observations that are there guiding you through your days. You will hear my own authentic accounts of blocked, stagnant days of struggle and how I learned to catapult myself forward, advancing to new levels of inspiration and manifesting. And you will learn how to integrate these techniques into your life so you can live a life of joy, peace, and fun adventures — reducing and eliminating any struggles with money, relationships, or health issues.

As you follow the techniques I share with you in *The Creation Guild*, you will master your craft of manifesting and begin to experience more inspiration, happiness, and synchronicities in your own life. Your inspired creations will soar. And when you encounter struggles and the rollercoaster of life takes you through the shadows and hills of your life, instead of wallowing in the dark areas, you will find yourself at the top of the next hill, full of trust and anticipation for the ride down the sunny side, waiting for the rollercoaster to catch up to *you*.

I invite you to come along to *The Creation Guild*, for the time has come for all of us to leave the struggle behind and learn how to refine the craft of manifesting the life of our dreams through the flow of our creative energy source.

We are all Creators.

Every single human on this earth
is a creator,
no one is exempt from this.

Every second of every day
we are creating.

Imagine the powerful flow that begins
when you create a space
to purposefully create.

The Beginning of this Journey: Why Am I Never Satisfied?

My Struggle With My Creative Self and the Push for More

I am sitting in my kitchen on a chilly morning in November of 2015. We have just had our first snowfall of the season, accompanied by a cold wind — not the soft, quiet snow-flakes that you welcome to cover the brown remains of fall, but a harsh, uncomfortable entrance of winter. It is prom-ising to be a sunny day, but the wind will keep it very cold. I am decidedly grateful that I do not have to rush out to work today. Today is a day that I can sit at my kitchen island, drink a warm cup of coffee and write in my journal. I have a few business details to take care of today, but for the most part, the day is mine to enjoy. Creatively, my first loves are painting and writing. These passions fill my soul with peace and fulfillment. My heart swells with gratitude as I think of how much I love days like this, when I can paint and write for hours if I want.

Then my mind flashes back to December of 2013, a time in my life when a day like this was unheard. As I allow the memories and feelings to flood back, it occurs to me how rapidly things changed. And so, it is with a growing awareness and clarity, like the glow of the early morning sun as it brightens the room that my mind meanders, and I am thinking back to where my life was two years ago and the practiced techniques I put in place to create this life.

I begin to list off all the changes that have formed in my life, and it occurs to me just how much I have learned about refining this creative process in my life. To create the life of my dreams, I have tweaked and fine-tuned the manifestation process over the last thirty-five years; however, in the last couple of years, I have re-committed myself to mastering the ability to harness this creative energy. I now have a much deeper insight and awareness of manifestation process and how to create the life of my dreams.

Let me start at the beginning.

In late 2012, I was stressed. Stressed and exhausted daily. I was pushing myself with a full-time teaching job, I had a direct sales business in health and wellness, and in the crevices of my life, I was building my own art business. I was the teacher, mom, bookkeeper, marketer, creator and everything else that goes along with that. My husband had his own business too, so I was taking care of his billing and paperwork. My mind was set that we would work hard for a couple of years and that everything would be set for life.

I was pushing for my dreams — to have the time and money to do whatever we wanted whenever we wanted, to own my dream home, to paint more pictures, to write books, to travel with my family and friends, and of course, to shop whenever I wanted to. I could easily picture this life in my mind's eye. I could see our three kids, each with the love of their life, in our beautiful new kitchen with a large island and granite countertops. My home would have large windows that let nature in, a wonderful art studio, lots of natural wood throughout, and a big stone fireplace. I could see both my husband and I there, enjoying this space with our family. I could see nice vehicles in the garage, lots of trees around us, and our dogs running around playfully. Visualizing myself painting in this space, and having a place to sit and write was easy. So with this vision in my mind, I was taking advantage of opportunities in earnest. Determination, or some would say stubbornness, kept me working hard.

My mother had always said I was a dreamer, and I was beginning to wonder if this was true. I was fifty and feeling too tired to go on. I was tired all the time, and it seemed that I was pushing my body too hard. This frustrated and disappointed me. Discouraged I would think, *maybe I will never accomplish everything I ever wanted in my life, maybe we are allowed dreams just to get us through this life.*

Sounds a bit like a mid-life crisis, doesn't it? Life at fifty was feeling very short. Why was I never content with what I had? Why was I always pushing for more? In other people's eyes, I had nothing to complain about. Surely I should have been happy with what I had. We owned our own home on a nice piece of property. Maybe it was not my dream home, and the kitchen was old and run down, and yes, the house desperately needed new windows, doors, siding, carpets and flooring, paint... in fact, the list stretched on to the point it overwhelmed me. But it was a good home, nicely built. It kept us warm in the winter, and was a beautiful, peaceful park-like setting in the summer.

There were lots of people who did not have that much. What right did I have to want more? And I was lucky to have been in love with the same man for over thirty years. We had a wonderful relationship and three amazing children who were grown and beginning their life paths. And, of course, I had my two steady companions, my dogs, Jack & Eddie. We had a great circle of friends, loving family back east and had had the opportunity to take a couple of vacations and do some traveling to distant locations — something we could *never* afford to do while the kids were growing up.

Life was good and we were appreciative and grateful for everything we had accomplished. We had worked very hard to get to where we were — healthy and secure with all the basic comforts of life. We had pushed through scarcity to create this place of comfort. We had been through all the challenges that life could throw at us: deaths of loved ones, bankruptcy, health challenges, poverty, abandonment, various life scares with our children that other parents can relate to, and both my husband and I had each survived different forms of childhood struggles in our past. There wasn't too much that people could talk about that we couldn't relate to personally. We had been in that *victim* role in life and were determined we were not going back there again for ourselves or our family.

Over the years, we'd worked together to build a life that gave us the security that an increase in finances brings and a strong love that bonded us all together. I was a teacher and loved teaching. It gave me a sense of purpose in this world, and I would look at the name on my classroom door with a sense of pride and gratitude that came from working hard to get to the place I wanted to be.

But I was burning out. Why? Why could I not do this? Other people did it just fine. I felt strongly that if it was meant to be, it was up to me. This was my motto. It gave me control. This gave me a sense of security. But I didn't understand what this statement truly meant — not yet anyway. We had created a life that, so long as we kept working hard, we could maintain and grow from there. But my heart was discontent, and I was tired all the time. The day to day pace was wearing me down quickly, and I had no time to paint. When I would sit to meditate, most of the time I would end up just falling asleep.

And so it went with 2012 giving way to 2013.

It was during the Christmas holidays of 2013 that I was able to sit down and contemplate my discontent. Why was I discontent? What did I really want? If anyone asked, I was fine. But I did not feel any excitement or even enjoyment in my days. Instead, I was exhausted and frustrated more and more often. There was so much work on my plate, I felt like I was suffocating. I knew if I kept it up, I would end up sick in some way. I knew that physically I could not keep going like this. But why could I not do this?

I would look at my friends around me with various demanding careers, and they seemed to be handling it just fine. What was wrong with me? I had these thoughts circling through my head all the time. In the past, I had a pattern of changing my career about every ten to fifteen years. Feeling restless if I was not learning or growing in some way, I would look to something new. Maybe it was more than that? I didn't want to change my career. I loved teaching. But I hated being exhausted all the time. It felt like my energy was being pushed and pulled in every direction, and it was draining me. My weekends were a game of catch-up, in work and sleep. But shouldn't I feel *replenished* if I loved teaching. Is it not supposed to fill you up if you are doing what you love?

And I missed being creative. I was so hungry to paint. After thirteen years of feeding my brain and working on my teaching skills and serving others, I just could not push down that creative side anymore. No longer would this part of me be satisfied with just a few creative outlets in the classroom. My soul was speaking to me, quite loudly actually. I loved the idea of writing — sitting in a quiet space in the morning with a cup of coffee, lighting a small candle in front of me, and just allowing the flow of words to pour through me.

I had become more and more negative. Even my husband had commented that I was not my usual happy self, and his comment shook me. That is not who I wanted to be, and it opened my eyes to the effect it was having on the people around me. People were pulling away from me. Wow! When did this start to happen? I had not even noticed until that moment. It was true.

But could I make the changes that would bring me back to my happy self? What would people say? I could hear the voices already in my head.

"What are you doing *now*, Janice? Why can you not be happy with what you have? You have worked hard to get where you are. Do not throw it all away now. What about saving for your retirement? You are risking your career. Your time will come, stay the course."

This drove me crazy! I refused to believe that you had to work all your life just for retirement. I refused to believe that life could not be what you wanted it to be. It couldn't be all about working hard just to pay off bills and prepare for your retirement. I was feeling choked with everything I had to do every day. I had struggled my entire life! This could not be what it was about.

At this rate, I would not *make it* to retirement!

On December 23, 2013, I sat down to create my dream mandala board. This is something I learned how to do about twenty years previous, and it was amazing how many things I had created in my life that were on my dream board. It held a lot of power, and I knew it. I sat quietly and gave all of this some deep, honest thought. I wanted to keep all my dreams of creating a beautiful home, enjoying wonderful vacations, and having a warm, loving circle of family and friends. But more than anything I wanted to feel peace, love, and joy every day. I just wanted to be happy again.

I drew my circle on my paper and drew myself in the center. All around me I wrote those words — peace, love, joy, trust, creativity, expand, beauty. I really wanted this with all my heart. I wanted to be happy every day. And so, these words filled my circle. Not the usual goals of physical manifestations, only the emotional longings of what I wanted. I did not care about the rest. I did not know how to get these feelings to manifest into my life. I could not see the path that it would take. I let go, with a small prayer in my heart.

"Show me the way."

I could feel my heart and soul expand as I wrote all my words in my mandala circle and put my intention very strongly into it.

And when you ask with clear intention and an open heart, it is given. Things started to shift quickly.

Now, almost two years later, I have created all those emotions in my life. And the physical manifestations have magically appeared along with them. I now teach only part-time, and my art business has grown to create an income that is almost filling the gap that came from my reduced hours. I have a beautiful new kitchen with a fabulous seven-foot granite top island that just screams "gather around me" every time our kids come for family dinners. Not only has my life improved, but there has been a ripple effect to those I love.

My husband is not working as hard, our kids have all found loving relationships, and my creativity has soared. My paintings and prints are selling in a steady flow. The words are flowing easily when I write. We have a fantastic new garage. And our daughter got married in our yard this past summer. I cannot express how magical that day was. Our family and friends traveled from eastern Canada to celebrate this day with us, and my heart was filled with love to see them all here in our home together. I have easily manifested money when it is needed. Resources just show up, and we always have whatever we need on a daily basis. We have abundance in all things. And I have learned to trust that this will always be there. And I am getting better and better at this.

What was the fine-tuning I did in these last two years to get myself here?

I have broken down my steps in the chapters of this book. This book will teach you a daily process that will help you create the life of your dreams, if you make it your intention and commit to making the changes necessary in your life. Life is not supposed to be hard. Life is not supposed to be filled with fear and hard work. These are things we have created because we lost the awareness of our own connection with a much more powerful force.

This force flows through you and is there for you every moment of every day, without any judgement of where you have been in the past, who you are, or what your religion is. It is simply a matter of changing your perspective and creating the space for your reconnection to — or communion with — your soul, something you can do in any moment. And when you do, your world will be rocked with the powerful changes that you can create. I will walk you through the process I have used so you can apply it to your life. And the greatest part is, it is all free, and no one is discriminated or judged unworthy. It is there for each and every one of us on this earth, and there is no lack in this flow. There is no scarcity. No one can take from anyone else's stream. There is more than enough for everyone. So let me help you begin your journey, and enjoy the process. Remember, we are learning more and more about this ability we have within us every day. Be gentle with yourself because, when you are critical with yourself, you step out of your flow of abundance.

We are all in this journey together. Let's get started!

If you want your life to change,
you must make the space
in your life to create.

I. It All Begins With You

To Change Your World You Must Make a Pact to Honor Yourself First

"You attract and manifest whatever corresponds to your inner state."

—Eckhart Tolle

If you are reading this book, you have come to a pivotal point in your life. Perhaps you are coming from a feeling of frustration, the feeling that enough is enough! Or maybe you are dealing with a health issue, a money issue, blocked creativity — what I call the black hole of creativity — or a feeling of being unworthy, unloved, or rejected, or maybe all of the above! Or perhaps you are content with your life but are a forever soul seeker, looking for the next key to unlock the door to your personal growth. (If you are, good for you! Imagine a world where we were all looking to better ourselves!)

Or perhaps you are like me and have been working on this 'creating your own reality' thing for far too long and have only had glimpses of it working in your life. The elusive manifestations that you want just seem to dance away from you each time you get close to them. But you are determined to figure this out and make it work more consistently for yourself! Well you are all in the right place. *The Creation Guild* is all about refining this craft of creation.

In 1992, I began to understand that our world is a manifestation of our thoughts, and I have worked on it every day of my life since then. I have read all the books, used positive self-talk and affirmations, meditated, done group work, circle work, energy work, many different healing modalities, visited high energy vortices on the earth, searched various religions, created dream boards and, among other adventures, studied under a shaman. All have helped me gain a better understanding of not only myself but how some of the universal forces work and the magical forces that are there.

There is so much to this world that we do not yet understand and so much more there than what we can perceive with our five senses. One thing I do know is that I may be gaining a much clearer understanding of the manifestation process; however, we are all continually learning and growing, and while I have much to share with you, I know in another year — or five years or ten years — we are all going to grow in leaps and bounds and will have so much more to share together. The timing is right for all of us to move past the struggle and enjoy a much more creative life.

Our ancestors have lived through some very difficult times, and their learning, growth, and perseverance was not for nothing. They have all helped build this world as it is today. We stand on the shoulders of our ancestors. And now we are at a pivotal point in history. It is time to move past the material struggle and hardship and transcend to a higher awareness, a more creative life. There is so much more to this life than just trying to meet our survival needs. Imagine the person you could be if you could just live each day, anticipating what new experience is coming and how you can contribute positively to your world, instead of droning through the monotony of a job you have to go to and do not really like, and being consumed with worries or stresses of the day. There is one thing I do know for sure, and that is what I am here to tell you.

You can have everything that you have ever wanted and more.

No one is exempt from this beautiful force. It is available to everyone and it is a copious well, never-ending in supply for each and every one of us. There is more than enough for everyone, and the more we grow in this direction, the more there is!

I am going to walk you through the steps of refining your ability to manifest the life of your dreams, so hold onto your hat because, by the end of this book, you are going to have experienced some staggering changes and will be on your way to a fun, creative life full of joy and love.

The first step to your new life is to make sure you are making a commitment to yourself. Just as Mahatma Gandhi said, if you want things to change in your life, you must be the change. You are the one in the driver's seat and have full control. You cannot keep going along doing the same thing and expect that something will happen and 'poof' you will be happy. There are still a lot of people who go day to day — whether consciously or subconsciously — with the thought that some outside force, like the lottery, will miraculously happen to change their life. Well let me tell you, miracles *do* happen, but not from an outside force. There is a strong force within you!

Keep in mind that this is *your* life. Not your spouse's, not your children's, not your family's, it is *yours*. This is it! And when we leave this earth, we leave alone, without any stuff to take with us. Each day we are here is a gift of life, and every day takes you closer to the end of this life on earth. Sounds a bit morbid, I know, but it is to your advantage to have this profound awareness of this gift of life you have been given. It is short, beautiful, and magical, and it is yours alone, and nothing and no one can change that. It belongs to you. If you want your life to change, *you* must make the space in your life to create.

And this is where we begin in this book; miracles *will* happen.

Coincidences, like being at the right place at the right time to bump into an old friend who just happens to tell you of a job opening up at their work that would be perfect for you... this will happen. Synchronicities happen that whisper to you along the way — *yes, keep going, you are heading in the right direction*. Creative inspiration will begin to flow to you like a dam was broken open. You will connect to something higher and magical. When you link arms with your creative energy source, you will hardly be able to believe the events that will fall into place for you — miracles. But first you must prepare the ground for the seed to take root. You need to take care of yourself, and make yourself the center of your attention with good self-care. The first step is to find your own happiness.

Why is taking care of you so important? Because, quite simply, this is your life. You are not here to serve anyone else, only to nurture your own self. Now at this point, I may be losing some of you who are dedicated servers in this world and believe your life is about making this world a better place and giving to others.

(Yes that is part of true spiritual happiness, and I will get there soon, so hang in there with me.)

You may be someone who thrives on giving to others, but if you don't know how to replenish yourself, you are going to burn out, and worse yet, manifest illness in your body. We are *source energy*. It is flowing through us freely and never ends. Nevertheless, we are experts at blocking this flow when we give too much attention to everyone and everything around us, and fail to focus on our own inner being. Too many servers of our world serve to the detriment of their own self. If you are serving, and it is *replenishing* your soul, you are on the right track. You need to tap into the heart and ask those tough questions of what really makes *you* happy. True courage is needed to make you happy first, regardless of what others think. If your automatic answer is "Yes I am happy serving others!" then think again. Spend some time finding the truth in your heart. No one else needs to hear the answer, just you.

Taking care of yourself, physically and mentally, goes hand in hand with your emotional wellbeing. You have heard this before, probably from your mother. But if you do not begin to include taking care of yourself as your biggest priority, you may as well stop reading right now. Each day your goal is going to be to feel good. That begins with how you feel physically, mentally, and emotionally. If you get up in the morning and do not feel well, and you know there are things you can do to change this, then you need to get on it.

Too often we put everyone else ahead of ourselves. Your priority focus needs to be on you. Raising children, taking care of the sick or elderly, can cast you into the role of martyr very quickly. And our society does not help. Selfish people are frowned on, and martyrs who drain themselves by giving all their time and energy to others are looked on as saintly.

(This is because those martyrs take the load off of the rest of us so we can be more selfish. Of course, we praise them. We do not want them to stop!)

It is easy to try and validate your existence with the thoughts of being needed. And I know many people that love to nurture and care for others. But it needs to be energizing, not draining. And it needs to be without any guilt attached to the caregiver at all. Our society seems to think there is something very admirable about the person who sacrifices their needs for someone else. This is distorted thinking. Yes, we need to provide a safe, loving, and secure home that meets the needs of our children. But so many men and women go far beyond this — often to the detriment of their own health.

I have been known to allow it to be my excuse for not taking care of myself too. It is easy to skip the gym, or to grab the fast food when someone else needs us *right away!* Our children learn by watching us. Our sick and elderly feel guilty and feel like they are a burden if they observe you doing this. Just like on the airplane when the flight attendant shows you how to put your mask on first in an emergency, before you help anyone around you, you need to replenish your *own* energy daily. Set an example, and honor our elderly. What do you want your children to learn? How do you want the people you are caring for to feel? Think back to your childhood and what you observed as the habits of your parents. We often take on our parents' work habits. But they lived in a different generation, and we need to embrace change in our world now. Be gentle with yourself and care for yourself the way you would care for your own child. Think to yourself, if this were my daughter or son, what advice would I give to them?

Eat foods that make you feel good, not just right now, but for several hours after you have eaten. Eat food that gives you energy, clarity, and vitality. This is a personal choice. You need to enjoy the food you are eating. This gift of our earth is bestowing sustenance upon you, and every person needs to think deeply on how the food they are ingesting is making them feel. Do not go on the latest diet because your friend did and lost weight. If you eat foods that you think are good for you, then they will be. Eat meat if you feel that meat is what makes you feel good. Be a vegetarian if that is what your heart is telling you. Become educated on what is in your food, but let your heart help you with your decisions.

Yes, you can use the excuse that eating that ice cream heaped with a chocolate brownie and caramel sauce is going to make you feel good right now and that that's what you really want. But will you still feel that way an hour after you eat it? This is not meant to make you feel guilty. That would be defeating what I am trying to get across to you. It is simply about you making conscious choices. So, if eating that scrumptious dessert is what you need right now, then do it, and do it by making a conscious decision and do not feel guilty about it later. The most important thing is that you do not beat up on yourself for what you are eating. Eating consciously means you are eating with awareness, deliberation, and intent. You are eating to feel good, physically, mentally, and emotionally.

Begin to take up any activities that energize you. Movement promotes energy flow. That is why dancing feels so good for so many people. You may go for more walks, go to a gym, join a class, take up yoga, or join a meditation class. It is important that you take time for yourself. Do not think about what you *should* do but rather what you would *like* to do, something that fires you up. Take up an activity that you are going to look forward to. Perhaps you just need to start with a few hours per week. If you do not get much time to yourself, then you need to set that time aside. Hire a babysitter for two hours one night per week and make that your time to just do what you want. This is not the time to go to the bar with your friends, but rather time to just be with yourself. This is your replenishing time. The time that you can totally open up to your source energy and just let it flow. Go for a bike ride or a walk. Take yourself out for ice-cream. Or join that writing, painting, craft, or language class you have always wanted to try.

I have been an artist for most of my life. And for many years, when I sat down to draw or paint, it was frustrating because it just would not work out the way I wanted. Art was a part of who I was; however, it was not integrated into *me*. There was my creative side to *me,* and then there was my everyday life. I did not know how to connect with my creative energy at that time, but fortunately, in spite of the frustration, I had enough passion for the activity that I continued to learn and hone my skills. It was not until a time when my son was experiencing a personal trauma, and as a family, we were struggling to get through this difficult time, that I started to paint from my soul. Any parent out there knows that, when your children are suffering, you carry that suffering with you. It is through our most difficult times in our lives that beautiful growth emerges for all involved. Well, this was one of those times that took me to my knees, searching deeply for guidance and understanding.

During this time of upheaval, my daughter and I were walking through a mall, searching for an outfit for her eighteenth birthday. We were both mustering up the happiness for her birthday, struggling as our hearts were breaking for her brother, for we were both feeling so helpless for him. We found ourselves standing in front of a gallery window with some beautiful paintings on display. They were full of color, movement and energy. They called out to my very soul and I could not take my eyes off them.

I stood before this gallery window and let out a deep sigh, and wistfully said, "Oh that is how I would so love to paint! It totally inspires me!"

Quietly my daughter looked at me and said, "Then why don't you?"

I turned and looked at her, and it was like a light bulb went off in my head. *Yes, why don't I? Why don't I?* It was such a simple statement that shook me to my core. I had studied the work of the Group of Seven, Vincent Van Gogh, Ted Harrison and Emily Carr and loved it. I had this natural flow and movement to the painting I was already doing. So I went home, searched this style of painting online and then began making it my own.

I had never painted with such joy!

I found peace and comfort while I was painting, even while thinking of my son's struggle. And I was completely energized! I could not get enough of it and delved into this new-found love of painting. I was painting just for me and for what felt good. I was painting from my soul! And when I finished six paintings I timidly put them up on social media to show to my friends.

They all sold within twenty-four hours.

I did not even put them up there with a plan to sell them, just share them. But people just jumped up wanting to buy them. And the rest is history. The ripple effect magically happened again. My son worked through his life-changing experience and grew into a strong, resilient man full of love and appreciation for family and a stronger integrity from his experience. We could not be more proud of him. And I was blessed with connecting to my creative energy source while I painted in a way that I am sure would not have happened without his contrasting experience. Our family grew closer and stronger, and I have now had the pleasure of selling my paintings and prints all over the world. Now I create for the joy of creation's sake. It is a wonderful feeling.

My point for sharing all this with you is this: this soul-filling feeling is what you are looking for. This can come to you just by walking your dog, or swimming, or playing a sport, writing poetry, singing, playing the piano, acting in a play or planting a garden. Do whatever makes your heart sing.

There is one more thing you need to do to help ensure you feel your best physically. You need to make sure you are getting enough sleep. I cannot stress enough how important this is. If you are going to feel good every day, it is difficult to accomplish this when you are dragging your butt around. Your patience with other people will be lower, and you will not be acting from your higher self. Sleep deprivation is a strong activist when getting sick. Your immune system lowers and erodes your ability fight off infections.

Too much sleep has been shown to have the same effect, so figuring out your optimum hours of sleep is key. Most of us know how much sleep we need to feel our best every day. However, it is important to know the placement of those hours also. I know my optimum hours of sleep for me are eight hours. When I go to bed at 10:30 p.m. and get up at 6:30 a.m. I feel energized and good all day, especially if I make this my continuous routine. As you become more and more aware of how you are feeling, you will notice even the slightest alterations in your body. This is the beginning of tapping into your own energy source in your physical body. Put your health first. Your goal, every minute of every day, is to feel good.

Most important of all — and you will hear this repeatedly throughout the coming chapters — taking fifteen to twenty minutes every morning to sit quietly, focus on your breathing and connect to your creative source energy, allowing it to move through you, is the best way to begin your day. In fact, it is the most important way to begin your day! You may need to get up an extra fifteen minutes earlier to fit this in, but it is vital to center yourself and feel that connection to your power before going out into the world.

I have learned how to connect during my meditation and feel that same flow of joy as when I am painting or writing. Meditation allows you to take a few minutes just for you. The silence helps you tune into your body and your life force. This is your time to be purely selfish and see yourself connecting to your energy source; allow the flow to move through you with your breath. I have found that visualizing myself out in nature while I meditate helps to stop all the mind chatter and to-do lists from running through my head. I have included a meditation in the back of this book that will teach you the basic process that I have used for the last twenty-five years, and it has worked beautifully for me.

When you first wake up in the morning, before you even get out of bed, train yourself to begin with a positive thought. See yourself as a cocoon of light and all around you is your creative energy source team of support. There is an energy of support that is there to help you in every way possible for this day. You are not in this alone. This energy expands with your successes and guides you on continuously, without any judgement at all. See yourself as this light force that is connected to your higher creative energy, which is you but a bigger much more powerful you.

That is your source.

The part of us that is here living out this earthly life is only a shadow of our higher self, but luckily we do have access to this higher power and wisdom at all times, and this is where all our answers are. Before you begin your day, check in with yourself; how are you feeling emotionally right now? See yourself connect to your source-energy and remember what your intention is — to feel peace and be happy.

Some days are harder than others. Be gentle with yourself. Do not reprimand or criticize yourself when you do not accomplish this. Just remind yourself of what you want in your heart and carry on. Create your own vision boards of emotions you want to feel and hang it up where you will see it every morning as you begin your day. You will be learning how to become aware of your thoughts and feelings throughout your days. State your intention for your day — your goal is to be happy and find joy and peace in the moments of your day.

Set yourself up by laying out a plan to follow through with as many of the steps outlined here as you can, and when life gets in the way or you fall off the tracks, simply get up and say to yourself, *I am doing extremely well, I am doing better every day. Tomorrow is another day. Right now, in this moment I choose to be happy.*

Key Notes:
- Enough is enough. It is time for a change!
- You can be, do, and *have* the life of your dreams.
- Self-care first; make a commitment to honor yourself.
- You are in control; it is your life.
- Eat to feel energized, vital, and good.
- Participate in activities that energize you and feed your soul.
- Get enough sleep.
- Meditate.
- Start your day with positive thoughts.
- Set your intention every morning.

Relaxing into play
will release the blocks,
and the gateway
will open.

2. Control Your Thoughts

You are a Beacon of Energy

"Everything we do is infused with the energy with which we do it.
If we're frantic, life will be frantic.
If we're peaceful, life will be peaceful.
And so our goal in any situation becomes inner peace."

—Marianne Williamson

When we look around us, there is so much happening in this world. Things seem to move very quickly, and our thoughts move at an even faster pace. We have trained our brains to process what we see, which in turn allows us to interpret the scenes and events around us in about a tenth of a second. This quickly translates to a thought and moves on to the next perception, again translating to another thought, and on and on.

Now the speed of our thoughts is an internal and highly individualized process, but it is estimated that we have up to 60,000 thoughts per day. I am sure we can all relate to our thoughts jumping from one subject to another. Have you ever had a thought and then stopped and tried to back-up your thoughts one at a time to understand how you possibly got to that point? It is interesting to observe how often our thoughts are directed by past experiences or events yet to come.

Consider this scenario:

Here you are driving down a country road on a beautiful morning. The sun is rising as you navigate your way to work for the day. It is a beautiful sunrise. The colors are stunning and are reflected in the scenery around you. Whether you realize it or not, your thoughts are flitting around, memories are bubbling up, at the same time you are wishing you could just take the day off to enjoy and skip work altogether. Oh, yes, *work* — that is another thought, and the day's events yet to unfold flash through your mind, while your emotions follow your thoughts like a shadow. You feel tired already just thinking about all you need to accomplish today, and all this reminds you how you are going to feel by 5:00 pm.

At this point you are reminded not to forget to stop at the grocery store after work. A list of needed items begins to rhyme off in your mind as you realize you forgot your grocery list on the counter *again*. Maybe you should pick up something to BBQ? Yes, that would be nice. And your mind now quickly connects to your family and how much they would enjoy this idea of having the first BBQ of the season. Now you are thinking about your home life and this triggers new emotional responses, as you think about the difficult discussion you and your spouse had the night before. You are worried about your oldest child and feeling a bit in the dark regarding their social life, with a nagging suspicion of their newest friend. And your thoughts are off in this direction.

Suddenly a deer leaps across the road.

Startled back to the moment you swerve, brake, and miss this creature by mere inches. Your heart is now racing as you realize what just happened. Your knees weakening in reaction, and you take a moment to breathe deeply hoping to regain your composure. You have been jolted back to this moment. Nothing else exists, not the future nor the past. You are breathing deeply feeling the rush of your blood. Coming back to this moment from all the ramblings of your thoughts a few minutes ago, you take in your surroundings once again. You look over to where that beautiful sunrise was happening moments ago and realize it has now crested the horizon and all the vibrant yellows, pinks and oranges have melted into a soft white and yellow glow. You missed the actual sunrise because your thoughts distracted you from the moment. The deer brought you back.

Now this is a typical scenario for all of us, even if your commute to work involves driving through the crowded streets of the city or commuting on a train or bus packed full of people. This happens continuously all day long. There are constant distractions throughout our day to take our minds this way and that. And we are often having multiple thoughts at one time.

What we do not often think about is that each fleeting thought passing through our mind — many not even recognized — happens in less than a second and each one is triggering an emotional response. Many of these emotions are based in our past experiences. And while we may have over 60,000 thoughts in a day, most of these thoughts are the same ones we thought yesterday! Our thoughts can be like a wild horse running this way and that through a field. It takes a concerted effort to rein that horse in to walk the path. And if we loosen up on the reins, the horse tends to stray off again and again until we get it well trained to stay the course. Becoming aware of our thoughts and recognizing where they come from — and why — is the first step to controlling them.

Now stay with me because here is the important part:

All these thoughts we have creating emotional responses in us average out to be our vibrational output that is pouring out to the universe like a signal on a radio tower. And as this signal beeps out in the universe it attracts the same frequency, bringing more of what we have in our lives to us.

Did you know thoughts create things? It is true, and this is how the Law of Attraction works. This is why our lives pretty much stay the same. If you are someone who loves drama, seeks it out and dwells on it, then that is exactly what you will get in your life — more drama. Now you may say you *don't* love drama, but it just keeps finding you.

Consider what your average emotions are in a day.

If you have a habit of replaying events of past hurts, neglect, abandonment or other events that you have had in your life over and over, and you talk about them with your friends, then you are keeping that energy of drama active in your life because, as you relive these events, you are reliving the emotions over and over. That is a strong radio signal that you are sending out as you talk about it. We *all* have stories of hard work, conflict, and sorrow in our past. Some of us more than others, but before you begin talking about your story, think about this: what is your purpose for bringing it up? Are you sharing this to gain a sense of belonging with the group you are currently hanging with?

Is it your ego that needs a bit of stroking? Do you want people to look at you and think, *wow they have been through a lot!* Thereby putting you on a bit of a pedestal? Be honest now.

I used to share my stories too. It helped me feel deserving of friendship and respect. I thought, if I could show people what I have been through, then they would accept and respect me. After all I am a survivor. But really, who isn't? Soon I began to realize that I was lowering my energy every time I talked about my struggles. And this was not helping me (or them) to raise our energy up to where I had grown to. All those struggles have been learning experiences with wonderful results coming out of them, but I do not want to emit that negative energy, I want my life to reflect happiness and freedom now.

Think carefully. What is in the story-telling for you?

Do you want to replay that signal? The only time you need to share these stories is to help someone learn from your mistakes. Sharing to coach someone or comfort them, giving them hope, brings a totally different vibration to the moment, and *that* is helpful. But sharing for your own needs of acceptance lowers the energy. This is because you are worrying about what they think of you — even though that is none of your business and perpetuates the cycle of that energy. Drama begets drama; anger begets anger, and so forth.

How do we make changes in our life? How do we get out of the stuck energy that has us continuously cycling the same life story? Here is what you need to do:

Control your thoughts.

It is that simple — *and yet, not that simple.* This is a skill that you need to work on every day and make your intention clear that you do not want negative energy in your life anymore. I learned a long time ago that forgiveness is just simply having selective thoughts. The same goes with drama. Stay on the positive thought train, and you can make big changes in your life. Every experience you have had in the past has brought growth and learning from it. If you can begin to see the positives from these times, then you are on the right track. I know sometimes it can be hard to move in this direction, as you may feel like a victim of circumstance, but you are only hurting yourself when you won't let go of anger or hurt.

Find the growth and strength you gained, and little by little, express your gratitude for what you learned. Just stop talking and reliving the negative events in your life history. Past experiences have helped you become who you are today, but they are like the foundation of your house. No one needs you to dig up the dirt around your house and show off the foundation. Think of all the positives that have come from those experiences. Make lists of these positive outcomes to help you move through any negative emotions until they become habits of thinking. You will truly begin to feel the gratitude in your heart for all those negative events and something else will grow too: your own self-confidence. You have made it through a lot of crap and here you are! You should be proud of yourself for getting to this point. Stand taller and stronger and let the person you have become speak for themselves. Just stop talking about it.

When you encounter people who want to share their drama with you, there are two things you can do. You can politely disengage yourself and remove yourself from the situation, or you can talk to them about the positives of their experience. Every single bad experience has the potential to bring positive growth and newness into your life. The more you focus on this, the less drama people will bring to you, and you will encounter these people less and less. This is the universe showing you your manifesting has begun.

Once you are manifesting a drama-free zone in your life. You will begin to notice that the people in your life who constantly have one dramatic event after another in their lives will slowly dissipate from your experiences. Have you ever noticed how heavy everything gets when you are with a group of people who share the same complaints as you do? You definitely do *not* feel better when you leave. It is nice to vent, at times, but in the end, what does it accomplish? Nothing changes from those kinds of meetings.

The teachings of Abraham–Hicks advises not to dwell on these negative thoughts for more than seventeen seconds. Because after seventeen seconds, like attracts like, and soon you will be on a roll of negative venting about everything in your life. Just let it go, and move on to something that lifts you up. You will find that you will begin to experience coincidental meetings with positive people, people who are also working on cleaning up their energy and thoughts and working on becoming more self-aware. This is your vibrational output shifting to new levels and attracting those same energies around you! Now you are attracting people who are at the same vibrational output as you. It is way more fun sharing with these new people!

Turn off the television. Television programming is all about drama and trauma because that is what sells. When you spend time watching these programs, your own thoughts and emotions are affected. As well, this hangs in your energy field sending out that signal again. Turn off the news. If it is urgent, you will hear about it. You need to work on focusing on positive things in this world and television rarely shows this. If you really need your TV fix, then watch information programming such as nature or science shows. A great comedy always lifts your energy too.

Let me be clear here, this does not mean that nothing will ever go wrong in your life again. Some of us need The Tower (that nasty card in the Tarot's major arcana that foretells of big changes coming) to show up in our lives, otherwise we would never move from where we are to the infinite potential of all that we can be. We are clearing away the old to make room for the wonderful new adventures and opportunities that the universe has lined up for us. However, there will be fewer and fewer events in your life that you consider worth getting upset over. As your perspective grows, so will you trust in your own ability to handle situations, and when this happens, the universe's propensity to bring good things to you will increase!

Keep thinking of your vibrational frequency as radio signals beeping out into the universe. Remember that thoughts and emotions create things. Refocus onto what it is you truly want to create in your life. Do you want to relive those old patterns again and again? Or are you creating a brand-new life, filled with your most precious dreams of what life has to offer you? Be gentle with yourself. When you find yourself heading down the path of negative thinking, just redirect your thoughts and pat yourself on your back for recognizing your actions. Let go of the past! We have all made mistakes. Each time you find yourself slipping back, refocus on something positive. Find the positive, and this will shift your perspective, thereby shifting your manifestations!

Key Notes:

- Become aware of your thoughts and backtrack to see why they came up.
- Each time you become aware that your thoughts have strayed, gently pull them back to positive thoughts that are in the moment.
- Each thought brings an emotional response.
- Let go of the drama in your life! You can create a life of adventure, fun, and abundance — choose to share *that* story!
- Make lists of the positive outcomes from every *bad* experience in your life.
- Remember, you are a beacon of energy vibrating out to the universe continuously — make sure your signal is what you want it to be!
- Relaxing into play will release the blocks, and the gateway will open.

Creating is a feeling,
not a product.
The product is the bonus.

3. Allow and Trust

Leaping a Hurdle: Creating is a Feeling!

*"The Universe is saying:
Allow me to flow through you unrestricted,
and you will see the greatest magic you have ever seen."*

—Klaus Joehle

Would it be reassuring for you to know that you have some amazing, extremely competent help out there? And that you can tap into this help at any given moment? You are not in this alone *and* no one is punishing you for *anything*!

This beautiful power at your fingertips is benevolent. In other words, it is *not* saying, "I'm not going to help you today because you are just not the person I thought you were. You can learn from this experience, suffer a little, and then maybe I will help you."

Your creative energy source is pure, non-judgmental, potential energy. It is pure, powerful energy. It is like a large bowl of soup just waiting for you to dip your spoon in. The soup does not care what you have accomplished or not accomplished, or the mistakes you have made in the past. It is simply there waiting to nourish you at any time you decide to dip in. The more you dip in, the more inspiration will come to you. You will have more to offer and more to give.

When our life gets so busy, we work hard to keep up with the pace. I do not know about you, but as my schedule fills, I lose that feeling of ease and connection I strive for when creating my life with intention. When I am stressed, I transform into a bit of a controlling fiend.

(Actually, my husband may say more than a *bit* of a control fiend.)

My mind moves into overdrive, and I find myself constantly problem-solving and planning for the next day, week, month, year, etc. I end up working at a pace that suddenly feels like a fast-moving treadmill, and I am afraid if I jump off, everything will fall apart. I've been described at times like this as being a bit intense and I forget to laugh — my kind friends say I am *focused*. Does that sound familiar for you too?

I know so many families struggling to balance careers, finances, children's schedules, activities and relationships. The pace of each day is 100 mph and is exhausting. When I am in this state I become *the fixer*.

"Don't worry, I will take care of that! I will fix it!"

Because that is the fastest and most efficient way to deal with issues as they crop up, and it is easier to make myself uncomfortable with the chore than someone else. I begin to take care of *everyone* around me, instead of allowing them the opportunity to solve their own problems. These are *my* issues of trying to manipulate and control my world. Letting go is hard for me, and life is a continual ebb and flow of being this way and then coming back into the trusting and allowing in the universe that is needed in order to create purposefully.

I am getting much better at it than I was, so I continually remind myself the universe is there to help and support me. I do not have to do it all myself! In fact, it is egotistical to think I can or *should*. There are much stronger forces and way bigger purposes to this life, and my measly little ideas pale in comparison of what could be happening. Tapping into my creative energy source brings much more clarity and beautiful inspiration, not just for my life but for *everything* around me.

One way I bring myself back into the *allowing* mode is by making a t-chart of my to-do list. This is one of the techniques I learned from Abraham–Hicks. I write everything that needs to be done by me today on one side, and a list of everything I can assign to the universe to take care of on my behalf on the other side. When I finish my list, my side is usually short and simple. I simply need to get connected to my creative flow and *BE*. On the universe side of things, the list is full of much bigger issues that I want to be taken care of.

Here is an example:

My To Do List	Universe To Do List
Meditate	Find money for tax payment
Take dogs for a walk	Find money for Visa payment
Call parent and schedule meeting	Line up a publisher for my book
Teach today 8am - 4pm	Brainstorm ideas for next chapter
Pick up water & milk after work	Summer holiday ideas
Go to yoga	Resolve that work/family/ friend issue

These bigger issues, that are on the universe's side of the T-chart are the ones that continuously roll around in my mind, creating constant clutter and taking away my clarity and flow. Getting them down on this list helps remove them from my mind and maintain clarity throughout the day. I do not have the money for the tax or visa payment today, so I am going to just let that go for the day and put it out of my mind. My focus will stay on *my* side of the list.

The first two on my list are manageable. I can get up and meditate then take my dogs for a walk. Not too hard to do that. If I have consciously put all the other issues out of my mind, then when I am walking my dogs, I will be with them, in the moment, enjoying the scenery and fresh air around me, allowing my creative flow to pour through me. When I am teaching my students, I will be in the moment and with them completely, able to meet their needs without the distraction of my personal problems. Any time throughout the day, if I find myself thinking about those bigger problems that need to be handled, I just remind myself, *Oh yeah, the universe is handling that today.*

My biggest job is to stay in the flow and keep my connection strong with my creative source. And what happens when I do this? It's interesting — someone tells me about this great vacation they had last summer and suggests I look into it. Or an advertisement comes through my twitter account of a publishing contest. The universe is taking care of its side of the list for me, and everything just falls into place. Maybe later in the week, I sell one of my paintings and now my bills are being taken care of too. The money always comes from some unexpected source. Then that work, family, or friend issue suddenly de-escalates and resolves itself without me having to do anything.

Things always work out when you stay in the moment each day with peace and happiness in your heart. It is like the day is paved out for you and you just need to walk on, take in the scenery and enjoy. There is space here — space for breathing, smiling, appreciating. And it is when you are walking the dogs or washing the dishes, staying in that peace, when suddenly an idea, solution, or inspired thought comes to you! You are more open to the flow of your creative source energy.

Starting your day off in the flow is vital. You get to set the theme for the day. You can either get up, rush around getting ready, and run out the door, reacting to everything that tumbles across your path, or you can get up with clear focussed intention of how you want your day to be. You set the pace for your day and the conditions around you. This does not mean controlling everything around you. It is about recognizing there is no *need* for control, simply allowing a powerful, positive presence of energy to flow through you.

To do this you need to take a few minutes to connect with your creative energy source and feel that life force moving through your body. Take the time to commune with that source, and then it is much easier to keep coming back into that space when you feel yourself slipping away. When that is the feeling you begin your day with, then it is easier to call up that feeling throughout your day. We do not always nail it every day. Being in this flow takes intention, commitment, and practice.

However, you cannot afford to *not* be communing with your creative source. This is your life force, and there is nothing else more important than nurturing this relationship. When you experience the sensation of what it is like to be in direct connection with your source energy, you will want to make it your goal every day. It feels warm, supportive and comforting, and you will not want to let anything take this feeling away. Fears and anxieties slip away and are replaced with a fullness that leaves no room for doubt. Nothing else feels this good, and being in this stream of energy makes all your experiences in life so much more beautiful.

You will hate it when you slip out of this connection. It's important to realize that you will feel yourself moving in and out of this flow all day long — don't be too hard on yourself when you have had a bad day. We all have those days, and that is okay. There will be days when you will feel so far away from this connection you will wonder if you ever felt it or it was just your imagination.

Be easy with yourself. Remember you are always connected; there is never a time when you are *not* connected. You just stand in the direct flow more at certain times than at other times. Learn to recognize when you have stepped out of the stream and take the steps needed to bring yourself back into alignment. Do not try to force anything, it will come back to you, and you will get better and better at this — there will come a time you can pull yourself into your source even at the same time you are standing having a conversation with someone. Remember, intention, commitment, and practice.

You are now probably wondering exactly how do you bring yourself back into feeling the full flow of your creative source? Can you recall that feeling you get on your first day of holidays? That feeling of completely letting go? You flop down into the lounge chair with such a feeling of lightness, knowing you do not have to do anything at all.

There is such a feeling of freedom knowing you can focus solely on doing whatever it is you want to do. All demands are lifted! *That* is the feeling you want to strive for every day.

Imagine you are a child again and all you have to do is play because your parents are going to take care of all your needs. Now some of you may be thinking this is not a very responsible way of living. But I promise you, it is much more responsible than the way you have been living. And all that stress and worry is not doing you any good at all. It is just cluttering up your mind and taking away your peace and joy in the moment. After all, whose words are those in your head that are saying you must work harder? Who is it chiding you to get your head out of clouds and start acting like an adult?

Those are not the words of your *higher* self — those are the words of fear. Fear of not keeping up, of missing out, of being judged by others. Fear of letting other people down. So just give this a try for a little while, and see how it goes. It does not need to be forever. Just a little while to see what happens. If you decide this is all for the birds, you can easily go back to your scurried, controlled, and stressed-out life. Remember, be gentle with yourself. Be easy and indulge in these feelings of letting go. One day at a time. Take a deep breath and remind yourself, *today I will only focus on my side of the to-do list.*

As each day goes by — while you are working on being happy and feeling good — you will begin to notice changes.

The first change you notice is that you have begun to feel better. Your worries have started lifting. When all you have to do is work on feeling good every day, there is less and less to stress over. Things are just falling into place each day. You are beginning to recognize that you have spent way too much time and energy trying to control the events in your day. Take things a moment at a time, a day at a time. Notice how everything just seems to happen in the right order. You are beginning to trust your instincts just a little more. When you feel yourself trying too hard, or pushing against something, be *aware* of it, and remind yourself what your goals are — then breathe deeply and let go. The first step is to *allow* yourself to feel this way. Just take a couple minutes every morning while you are doing your daily meditation, and call up this feeling of completely letting go.

When I first began understanding this idea, I had a dream that there was an older grandfatherly man in my life, and he was reassuring me that he would take care of everything. He reminded me that I could let go of the controls and he would handle it. It brought to mind the feeling a child has when they know their parent is going to take care of where the next meal is coming from, or where they are going for the day. Remember, you have a support team, helping out behind the scenes all along the way. And if you could just let go a *little* bit more, then, when things do work out, your trust in your team would increase.

Letting go was a challenge and took me a long time because there had been many times in my life when it appeared that my prayers went unanswered. Miracles did not seem to happen when needed, which is why I became a hard worker.

(If it is meant to be then it is up to me).

I did not have trust that the universe or *anyone* else would handle things, so I made sure I did. My husband had the same mindset, which is probably one of the reasons we got along so well from the beginning. We were both determined and hard workers. Hard work will get you a fair distance. But remember, you do not have to work so hard in life to have what you want. I understand now why those miracles did not happen. I was not allowing them to come. You need to focus every day, set your intentions, and work on those good feelings, eliminating as much of the worry and stress as possible.

Remember, everything always works out, even the tough stuff.

Trusting is the most important step in this whole process. When you can trust that your creative energy source is there — bringing the power of the universe and flowing through you — then you can hold the feeling, and the feeling is *vital* to manifesting. Here is a specific example of how I worked the magic of creating by allowing my creative source energy to flow and solve a struggle we were experiencing.

There was one time when we had a pretty hefty bill hanging over our heads. I had no idea how we were going to pay it. And this was a recurring problem in our lives — we'd get ahead, only to have a big bill pop up and drag us back again. I *knew* I was trying too hard, and it was time to let go and trust my creative source. And I also knew, by this point in my life, that creating the feeling was step one to manifesting it in a material way.

It happened to be the first day of my summer holidays, and I had a quiet weekend in my yard planned. I imagined what I would feel like if that bill was just taken care of. How would I feel if it was not hanging over my head anymore? What if someone magically swooped in and took it away? Suddenly I could feel that peace flowing over and through me.

Oh, that would be so wonderful, I thought. *I would feel light and free and like I truly was on a holiday on some beautiful tropical beach. I* could feel it so strongly inside me that my heart felt lighter already, and I decided I was going to make sure I held onto that feeling all weekend.

And I did.

All day, every day of that long weekend, I imagined that bill was gone — taken care of — never to worry about again. After three days, the feeling faded, but I went on with my week and put my faith in the universe. I knew that somehow — I did not know how — but *somehow* that problem bill would work itself out. I kept repeating to myself, *I have no idea how, but somehow it will all work out.* And I would put it out of my mind again.

If I found myself worrying at the edges about it, I just imagined the old man in my dream was working on it and that the solution would be revealed soon enough. Within two weeks, it was brought to our attention — through a letter in the mail — that we actually had the exact amount of money we needed to pay off this looming bill via a life insurance savings policy! We did not even know there was money sitting in that policy for us! It had been sitting there for about ten years, and we did not realize we could access it! And I had been under the assumption that there was nowhere, I mean *nowhere*, we could get the extra money from for this bill! Miracles do happen.

As these big or small miracles happen more and more in our lives, our trust builds up bit by bit. Now to me, this was no small act and was *exactly* what I needed to build my trust up in a big leap. But as little things happen each day, you begin to realize that maybe there is something more out there helping you and that you are going to be just fine. Certain things begin to happen in your life that just seem to be a bit more than coincidence, more like synchronicity, some powerful force is at work.

Perhaps you get a flat tire and a tire shop mechanic just happens to be driving by and stops to help you out. Or you meet up with the right person at the right time who gives you the information you needed to solve a problem in your life. Or someone you have been thinking about and wanting to talk to calls you. Or a gift is given to you with exactly what you need. Or a conversation inspires a thought in you that makes you excited to take action.

And you will begin to recognize that there truly is more to this world then what we know. And maybe, just maybe, you can learn to trust in the fact that you do have help available to you if you can simply fine-tune your awareness. And if you can hold onto that feeling of already having your problems solved, then you can trust that things will come together perfectly. And miracles will begin to happen for you. Regularly.

Key Notes:
- Open space and create ease that will allow you to be in the moment by creating your to-do list and a list for the universe to handle.
- Begin each day with a meditation to establish your connection before you meet the world.
- Bring yourself back into the feeling of letting go throughout your day through your imagination. (Recall the feelings of freedom when you are on vacation.)
- Creating is a feeling, not a product. The product is the bonus.

- Build up your trust by noticing how the universe is working for you. Notice even the smallest events that happen to bring you just what you need.
- Trusting and holding the feeling is the key to manifesting. Keep repeating to yourself, *I have no idea how, but everything will work out*. And hold onto the feeling of freedom and happiness.

Being in survival energy sucks.
We manifest the struggles in our life
to help bring clarity and expansion
to our creations.

4. Moving Out of the Survival Energy

Spending Time with Your Heart

*"From my obscurity came forth a light
and illuminated my path."*

—Kahil Gibran

After the first writing of this book, I worked on each chapter, slowly refining, shifting and elaborating the words while editing in the process. I worked slowly, contemplating, allowing the words to develop and grow each day. I would sit in meditation on the topics and observe the events of my days to add more meaning. When I reached this chapter — which was originally titled Solitude is Addictive — I hit a wall.

It was January, and events had unfolded in my life, making writing a struggle. Both my health and finances were taking a downward spiral. I took some time to work on these, but nothing seemed to make a difference. By March, I was feeling like I was in a black hole. I was struggling to understand what this was all about, and I was working diligently on fixing it. I did everything I knew to get back into my creative flow, but nothing was working. Oh it would work for a short time, but then I would be back down in the hole again. What the heck? What was going on? How could I write a book about manifesting if I could not pull myself up and manifest myself out of this mess?

It is easy to manifest and be in a place of gratitude when everything in your life is going great. Wouldn't it be nice if we were all millionaires living in vibrant health with the love of our life? Who would not be happy and full of gratitude? The real rub is when you are in a place of survival and you are trying to manifest yourself out of it. I was clearly reminded of this as I was writing this book.

I have been in this survival place before in my life. In fact, financial abundance, or the lack of it, has been a big part of my life story, right from childhood. As I mentioned in the introduction, I have worked very hard to get away from that life of scarcity and it *can* be accomplished, to a degree, through hard work and perseverance. But this was all at the cost of my health and losing my connection with my creative soul.

I had started this journey, determined to prove — first to myself, then my kids — that life does not need to be constant struggle and hard work. And after putting my practices to work in my own life, and experiencing my shift to one of joy and abundance, I wanted to share this with everyone around me. It saddened me to see people in my own community struggling so much.

I remember one day watching people walk by in big chain store, observing how they were living from a life of hard work and disappointments. Clarity and empathy surged through me as I watched people pass by me. You could easily see the light in their eyes was dull. Life from their perspective was so hard and had trodden them down. Their dreams had died. I knew that it did not have to be this way, and it saddened me to see so many souls living day to day without much hope.

I felt strongly in my heart that you can create the life of your dreams. I knew, down to my very core, that you can be, do, and *have* what you want. You can wake up each morning excited to see what the day will bring, instead of waking up with fear and anxiety, anticipating more problems that are sure to come. I had experienced joy in each day. And then, in the middle of writing this book, I was reminded how hard it is to believe this, to trust and open to the power of the universe when you are in the midst of survival.

When you are in survival energy, it sucks. There is no better word than that. It is choking. It is suffocating. And it is heavy. It is hard to be creative and pull in those feelings of freedom and happiness that I talked about in Chapter 3. It is hard to be grateful when you wake up in the morning knowing you have to come up with some money today or the hydro guy is coming to cut your electricity off. It is hard when you feel anxiety clench around you every time your phone rings because you know the bill collector is looking for your next payment, and you do not know what to tell them anymore — so you just let it ring, and ring, staring at the phone until they hang up.

I have even experienced the feeling of paranoia thinking that maybe I was being followed as I drove my business van around the city, worrying because I was just about three months overdue in my lease payment. I was sure they would track me down to repossess this vehicle that I desperately needed to continue my business and bring more money in. I have felt the bleakness, humiliation and dishonor that come with all of this and coming to the realization we were so far down that the only option was to claim bankruptcy. Not a pretty place to be.

I thought I had remembered all of this clearly. And I had in my mind. But in order to write this chapter, and this book, and connect to my readers, I had to feel it again in my heart and in my body. I had moved past these experiences in my life, but I had tucked it all away carefully, making sure I never had to go back there again. I would not let my mind go back to it. I did not even like to talk about it. I would just put it away, change the subject, because how can this help me now? What use is it to drum up those feelings? I want feelings of lightness now, abundance, joy and excitement for fun new adventures. As I said in Chapter 2, I just wanted to let the drama go!

But I had been manifesting writing a book with an authentic voice, wanting to reach out to each person with my heart, to help them shift their life as I had done. And my creative source heard my request, allowing me to delve back into those feelings.

Yes, it is very difficult to manifest when you are worried about survival. I remember now, how I did not feel gratitude in my heart when I had only twenty dollars for groceries for the week and had three kids to feed. I remember struggling to find food for their school lunches. I remember them telling me what *other* kids took for lunch and how they wanted that too. I remember the feeling of shame that I could not do that for them. It is much easier to fall into anger, resentment, depression or feeling victimized instead of feeling grateful that I could give them a peanut butter sandwich.

So now, as things in my life quickly turned from rosiness to survival once again, I fought hard against it. I remembered what it was like, and I was *not* going back there. We were sinking. Work was hard to get for my husband, the oil field work had dropped off, and this was affecting every industry in the province, causing many others around us work shortages also, and our savings got eaten up in just a few short months. I was reminded clearly what so many others were going through economically.

All the old fears and memories were triggered. Bankruptcy, losing our home, moving to a place we did not like, losing control of our lives and losing our power. *How can I be writing a book about manifesting the life of your dreams if I cannot get myself out of this black hole of survival energy?* This is such a familiar place for me that it almost felt comfortable. This survival energy is genetically ingrained into all of us, and we are incredibly prone to continually move back into it. This is where we have come from for hundreds of years. Our ancestors, grandparents, and parents have lived this energy. They lived through two world wars and the depression. This energy of despair and survival was part of their lives and so it fed down to us.

Each day I worked diligently, trying to reconnect to my creative flow. And it would work *temporarily*, but then I was back down again in that heavy sludge. I was not able to work through this on my own. Sometimes you need to show your vulnerability and truth. I am not invincible and cannot always go it alone. And this is where I let go and gave up. I allowed myself to sink and wallow in the darkness for a couple hours. Then I knew what I needed to do. I knew I could not do this alone.

It was time for me to connect fully with these fears, so I opened myself to them. And I called my beautiful friend, Melba, to help me through this process. Sometimes, you need to reach out to the angels around you to work through the muddy parts instead of wallowing in them. I needed this life pattern to get worked out. And we did it. We talked, I cried, we cried, and we came through it with clarity and appreciation — our hearts both full of love and gratitude.

Melba helped me go back to those difficult days. After all, she was there beside me while I lived them. I reflected on my life. I went back to the struggles and joys and the lessons and all the wisdom that came from it. I realized I was blocking out, squeezing my heart closed in an attempt to protect myself from experiencing it again. Having an open heart is vital to creating with inspiration, so I just allowed it to flow through me.

I wanted this book to be written with an authentic open heart. To do this, I needed to delve back into those hard feelings. *Manifesting is about feeling.* And our manifestations grow as we grow. I had to be willing to go back into that survival energy and appreciate it fully in order to grow into my bigger feelings of abundance. And I needed to be reminded what so many people are experiencing day to day, so my words may be able to take their hands and walk them out of it.

Reflecting back through my life, I saw myself as a young girl meeting her first true love. I saw us getting married and growing our family together. Clearly, I saw our struggles to hold onto our first home, when the kids were very young, I also saw all the love and laughter in that home. There were so many lessons that came from those struggles. So many friendships were developed during that time. That is when

I met my dear friend Melba. She moved into the house next door to us.

That was thirty years ago now. Treasured friendships come during hard times. And there were others too that I hold close to my heart. I felt so much gratitude swell up in my heart as I thought of all that love and those friends. I then thought of my kids, and the memories of raising them in that house flashed through my mind. Gratitude for being able to raise three beautiful children and see them grow into adults moved through my heart and body. It was during that time I started a much more conscious spiritual search and the meaning for life, for my life. Where would I be without that?

Gratitude again expanded my heart. Gratitude for my spiritual search that started during those struggles thirty years ago, gratitude for all I have learned from it. The gratitude for my own learning and growth through job after job that I held and which led to my teaching career. My heart expanded as I thought of more friends and family that encouraged and supported us through the years, through the bankruptcy and loss of our home.

I thought of our move out west, full of hope for a new life for our little family built on new opportunities. The loss of my mom to cancer and the gratitude of all the lessons I learned from her. The separation from friends and family and how it forced us to grow and become stronger and bond as a family. I realized it was during the most intense times in our lives that my creativity grew stronger, and if I let it flow, beautiful things emerged. I knew this was my developing connection to my creative source.

I could feel the gratitude in my heart now. I was feeling so grateful for everything in my life. Even our current struggles now were beginning to make more sense to me. I realized these new struggles were temporary. We were different people with so much more wisdom. This too would pass. And we would be just fine, no matter what happened.

Everything always works out.

I could see clearly that creating was like standing on the edge of a cliff. We are standing with our toes on the edge and there is infinite potential swirling around in front of us. We need the faith and trust to step forward and, as we place our foot, the earth manifests beneath it. Behind us are all our ancestors building the platform for us, and they continue to send their energy and take joy in our creations, encouraging us to move forward with confidence.

And so, as we move forward, it is important to reflect on our past not with anger or fear of repeating experiences in the future, but appreciation for the lessons we have learned and the strength we have gained from it. We need to open our hearts. Feel that expansion of the heart in our body fully. Let go, be authentic to yourself, feel with your whole heart and body all your life. And feel your connection with each other. This is a journey we are all taking together, even if it is an individual experience.

Many times you may have a big wad of resistance that is getting in your way, as I did. Thoughts are rolling and tumbling around in your head, and they will not stop. It is like the recurring dream you have when you are battling a fever. It just will not stop, you wake up, and every time you fall back to sleep, you go right back into that same dream again, over and over. When we are worrying about a problem in our lives, it is very much like that. Fear closes our hearts, constricts it and chokes us off from all that is around us and available to us. There are ways to release this, and once it is released, you will feel a huge weight lifted from your shoulders. It may be a problem you are trying to find a solution to, or a repetitive pattern in your life that keeps playing over and over again. Whatever it is, you need some relief from it. So here are three steps that can help you clear your heart and body of this stuck energy.

Three Steps to Release
1. **Set your Intention** — You need to *want* to release it. This needs to be your clear intention. You want to find peace in your heart. Your number one goal is to feel good again. You are tired of carrying this weight around and want it gone. You are sending out a clear intention to the universe that you have had enough and are ready to grow and move on from this experience.

2. **Let go of the ego** — You need to open yourself up to all possibilities. For me, I needed to be open to receiving help. I was so determined to figure this out on my own and was letting my ego get in the way of finding my release. Our ego is sneaky and can wheedle its way into our problems without us even realizing it. So be ready to say, *I am wrong, I need help, I can change*.

3. **Open your heart & body** — Melba was a safe place for me to talk through my struggles, and she helped open my heart by showing me that my feelings were completely valid. This was important for me because, as a compulsive do-it-yourselfer, I often feel there is something wrong with me when I cannot do it myself. I am continually reminded that we humans are all the same; we all go through the same feelings and often

the same thoughts and I am not an anomaly. This is very reassuring. I relaxed and followed her reflections back to all the wonderful experiences and events in my life.

You need to find a way to relax and stop beating yourself up over your struggles. Many of the techniques I outline in this book will help here. Meditating, walking in nature, holding a baby, petting your dog (or cat), journaling, going to the gym all work. But if they are not working, then it may be time to find someone to talk with. Melba is a Rubenfeld Synergist. This is a person who helps others become aware of the mind/body connections and helps them work through areas of their life that feel stuck. I am lucky she is also a best friend and confidante. However, I have in the past had a few visits with other psychologists to work through issues that have kept me stuck in repetitive patterns. This is often the safest way to get a non-judgemental, trusting voice to walk you through these parts of your journey, and I highly recommend it for those that are truly seeking self-actualization and continued growth. You will feel your whole body relax and your heart expand and release as you move through this process.

After my talk with my friend Melba, I spent time alone, reflecting and writing. Are you comfortable with being by yourself and working through your deep thoughts? You need time to absorb and tuck your new awareness into the spaces of your soul. Sort of like patting down the pie dough into a nice neat pie plate, making space for all the rich berry filling. This is a very personal journey. This is *your* journey. It is a journey we take alone, but the funny thing is we all share the same journey! We just take different paths.

You can read these words, but you cannot truly understand them until you have lived your own experiences. Living and experiencing them in your heart is what gives meaning to all these words. Words, although helpful to prepare us a bit, just do not interpret accurately — true understanding comes from the actual experience. And living a rich and textured life comes from experiencing every aspect of life and appreciating every moment. So be comfortable with working through your struggles, be honest with your feelings, and also be comfortable with being alone to work through them. Have an independent adventure in this life!

Key Notes:
- It is easy to practice gratitude when everything is great in your life.
- Life happens and we need to keep moving forward, learning and growing.
- Being in survival energy sucks! Your manifested struggles help you move forward in growth.
- There is so much to be grateful for in our life struggles — find the gold from the challenges presented to you.
- You must open your heart and feel in order for your manifesting to grow.
- When you are stuck with a wad of resistance follow the *Three Steps to Release*.

You will find
your creative soul connection,

when you slow down
to the heartbeat
of the earth.

5. Attracting it All

Finding the Love of Your Life!

"The quieter you become, the more you can hear."

—Ram Dass

Slowing down and taking time for our own self needs to be a priority if we are going to be creating a life with intention. This world is moving very fast, and we are not meant to move that quickly. Our soul moves to the rhythm of the earth's heartbeat. And when we quicken ourselves beyond that, we can sustain it only for a little while — eventually we will hit a wall. This may be a wall of exhaustion, illness, perhaps a serious disease, or a traumatic event that manifests to bring your attention to the moment.

You may be experiencing a time in your life right now when you begin to question all the choices you have made up until this point. You may be questioning the direction you can see your life heading. You may question why you are doing what you are doing every day. What is your purpose? How do you find your purpose in life? You will find your creative soul connection, when you slow down to the heartbeat of the earth.

As you begin to put into practice the guidance in this book, you will find a peace that comes with your alone time. Those quiet moments of contemplation and meditation are creating gentle shifts in your life – showing incremental signs of balance. Your life is beginning to quiet down. There is less chatter in your mind, less of the mental arguments and more of clear intention.

When I begin my meditation, especially if life has been a flurry of hustle and bustle, it reminds me of being at a very loud, busy party with lots of people around and quietly slipping away going down the hallway to be alone. You find a quiet study or office and gently close the door. The voices and laughter are muffled, and you take a deep breath, reveling in the quiet. No one has noticed you slip away, and you are peacefully alone, just taking a breather before you go back out to join in the fun. It is a calming feeling.

The truth is you need to be in silence to hear the wisdom of your inner soul. You need to pull away from the crazy energy, fast-paced stimulation of our world. There is so much clamour and noise out there all the time. We do not realize how much hubbub and stimulation is around us all the time, until we slip away to a few moments of silence. Similarly, you can go out of the city, into the country, forest or mountains and feel the energy shift. The silence is peaceful, devotional. Soon you will hear the sounds of nature that you did not hear before. It slowly creeps into our awareness, but it is a very different energy from being in the city. It is the soul of the earth that you hear.

Our cities are a conglomeration of high-powered manmade stimulations — traffic sounds, cell phones, people talking, music, computers, televisions, handheld devices. It is more than what we hear with our ears; we also feel it in our energy. Not to mention the visual stimulation. Everything is moving, changing, shifting and constantly vying for your attention. Taking time for yourself away from these things brings you back to the sound of your soul.

At first it is difficult because it is hard to stop all the mind chatter. Your mind is moving at the pace of the world you live in day to day, so it will continue with that pace for a while. It takes some time to slow it down, but there are ways to do this even in the midst of all this manmade stimulation. One way to balance this is with daily meditation, as I have described in the previous chapters. However, the best way to slow down is to regularly spend time in nature or taking regular vacations. Being in the mountains is one of my favorite places to be. As you walk through the trees, you feel like you are slowing down to the heartbeat of the earth. You may find this on a mesa in the desert, a beach near the water or your own backyard or porch watching the sunset. You become more grounded to who you are and what is important in your life.

We have all had that feeling when we take a holiday spent in nature — a forest, a beautiful island retreat, at a lake or in the mountains — and all of a sudden you let out a big sigh. You let all the air out as if you have been holding your breath and all the tension releases. This may happen as soon as you arrive, or after three hours, three days or three weeks. It takes time to reach this space, and you cannot force it.

I know I have been on a vacation and, after a week, I say, "Oh I am so relaxed now."

Then after another week I think, *Wow I thought I was relaxed last week but now I am even more relaxed!*

This is when you are beginning to feel the earth's heartbeat and you have slowed down, syncing up to it. Your whole body responds to this. You can feel your soul connecting, healing. Peace floods through your body. The earth begins to work her magic and heal your tattered soul. What seemed complicated before now becomes clearer for you, and with this clarity comes value. Your heart knows the answer to everything that you want, and it is only in this peace that the answers come to you. Why is this important?

Here is what you need to know;

Because this new found place where you strengthen your relationship with your creative energy source is where your creativity is inspired, and through nurturing this relationship, expansion begins.

Being immersed in our world is stimulating, exciting, and allows many opportunities for us to contribute with purpose to life and the people in it. We can give to this world in beautiful ways when we stay connected to our creative energy source. However, when you don't take the time to center your soul, you will find life gets more difficult, problems and complications arise, roadblocks pop up, and our bodies suffer.

When I give in to the workaholic side of me, not taking time off to replenish, after several weeks, I feel like the energy surrounding my body has been pushed, pulled, poked and scratched, and I need time to heal it before going back out there in the world. During these times, I instinctively know that if I do not find a way to regroup then I am going to get seriously sick. If I am in constant protection mode, I cannot expand, give to, and enjoy the people around me.

I love my work as a teacher, writer, and artist. I know, from past experiences in corporate jobs, that working in a fast-paced, highly competitive workspace filled with mistrust among your colleagues takes its toll. These are difficult places to be, even if you love the work. Teaching is a job of high energy, for you are constantly *on* — it's like being onstage all the time. You cannot have a down or low-energy day.

You walk into that school, and you begin multitasking immediately. Your awareness needs to be alert in all directions. Every moment is a teaching moment, and there are always lots of emotions in a middle school. You are on high alert to the needs of twenty-seven or more kids under your care. Now I am not saying teaching is any more difficult than any other job. There are plenty of much more demanding careers, such as in the medical field or other high demand service industries. I cannot imagine being paged from my bed in the middle of the night to go help an accident victim. My point is simply that we all impact other people — for better or for worse — mostly without realizing it, and it is our responsibility to make sure we are taking care of ourselves so our impact in this world is positive.

I see all of us as cocoons of light as we move through our days. Our light mixes and passes through the light of others all the time. If we are not stable in our own connection, then we are all mostly floundering in a sea of energy. Imagine if we were each strong and connected to our own flow. Then when we interacted with others, we would strengthen each other and become an immense force. The more we connect positively with each other the stronger our light shines.

In *A Course in Miracles,* it says we gain our healing through our brother. We help each other grow and learn, we are in this together. *We* are many times each other's angels. But first we need to connect with our own inner soul and recognize we have this creative energy source, this light within ourselves, only then can we see it in others. We are having a shared experience created jointly with other souls, but if we go out into the world without a strong connection to our own source, we are not helping anyone, and we contribute to some of that chaos, even unintentionally.

Connecting to your creative source energy will help you become more aware on a daily basis. You will begin to ask yourself questions. What do you want? What are your core desires? What is calling to you? What are those deepest feelings that drive you through life?

I think I needed to be a workaholic to find my soul. I pushed myself to the extreme limits to be a success and realized that that was not where I was going to find my satisfaction or happiness. I would argue that I was happy with my life, but I just wanted more money and the security that came with it. I wanted to be a successful business woman so I could gain respect from everyone around me. But in the end, I realized these were empty desires. And success is elusive and totally subjective. I needed to hit the wall of exhaustion to finally realize that I did not want to work that hard in my life! I needed to find my deeper connection.

I had always been a spiritual seeker, even from the young age of seven years old. But I had lost myself and my purpose for a little while. I remember the morning it hit me like a great epiphany. I was sitting in my car waiting for my

70 Janice Gallant

windows to defrost. My mom popped into my head and for some reason, and it was that moment that I realized my mom was not much older than me when she died. And I thought, *if I only had a few years left to live, would I be doing this right now? Would I be heading to this job that I say I love? If I only had a year to live, what would I be doing right now? If I only had ten years to live, what would I be doing? What have I not experienced in life yet?*

What was my bucket list?

If we were to live each year as though it was our last, I think we would all become a little more selfish with our time and energy, finding a deeper sense of peace and happiness along the way. We would stop living our lives to please others and begin to build a life of meaning. We would achieve clarity on what our core desires really are.

Remember we talked about responsible living? It is your responsibility to nurture your connection, control your thoughts, and recognize exactly whose words are rolling around in your head. When you begin to live responsibly, you are living authentically. Authentic living is about living from your soul. Your decisions and actions are no longer in the reactive mode. So much happens around us every day, and it can be very difficult to remain centered in your *self*. We get caught up in the rush of life, and suddenly we are not living anymore, we are merely reacting. This is not responsible living, on the contrary, it is very irresponsible. We need to learn to live each day in spirit, connected to who we truly are and allow our inner creative source to guide us with our actions and decisions each day.

We came to this earth for this wonderful experience of living a creative life, and every day is wasted when we allow the currents of life to push us around or just bob and float in the ocean of life instead of finding the flow of the water and moving with it. Have you ever tried to swim upstream or swim away from a strong current? It is nearly impossible. But when you turn and go with the flow of the water, you are suddenly much stronger and moving more quickly than ever. This is what connecting to your soul feels like — you are in a stronger flow of power. Thoughts and ideas freely flow to you. You are inspired to do things, like call that friend you have been thinking about, find a new job, write a song or poem, climb a mountain, write a book or take a dance class. Be brave and do whatever you are inspired to do! Welcome inspiration when it comes knocking on your door!

Do not waste the gift of each day. We are creators, and we create every single moment of our lives. There is a powerful force there to assist us, and when you tap into that divine energy, there is nothing you cannot do. We have this power within us, and now is the time for allowing this power to flow through us freely. Now is the time to act like the conductor of a great symphony. It can all come together perfectly. Imagine what could happen if you tapped into even the smallest stream of this power. This is the power — the life force — that created our universe. The same life force flows through and within us.

Make a commitment to this life; search for transcendence and capture the flow. This flow is so much stronger than anything you have ever felt in your life. You will not find anything more powerful than what is inside you. Here in this space, finally, fears dissolve, and there is security — the security you have been searching for in your life. Here, finally, is the intensity of love you have been searching for your entire life. It was always there within you, not in the outside world.

We can search as much as we want, but when we find security or love *outside* of ourselves, it is always temporary and conditional. It is never a lasting feeling, and then, when it fades, we are left feeling cold, empty and rejected. You will never find what you are searching for outside your own self. To be loved is wonderful, and everyone deserves it, but to find the love *inside* you is where the power is. When you find this source, your energy expands, and you open to the power of your soul. Everything in your life begins to fall gracefully into place.

Learning you can open to that power *regardless* of outside conditions will allow you to soar. You will find it gets easier and easier to do this as you practice it in meditation. When we achieve this then we begin to live authentically from our heart. And when we live from our expanded heart, it ripples out to all those around us, helping elevate them to find their creative source energy. Your energy expands, and the love you are capable of giving expands with it. Your relationships flourish. And you begin to manifest wonderful things in your life!

I have someone in my life who is very dear to me. And like so many others, I watch her react to conditions around her, constantly searching for love on the outside. She is a very self-aware person and knows she is doing this, but she still struggles to stop because life is moving too quickly. We have all experienced this, but she is aware enough to recognize it, and we shared our stories one day.

In a tender conversation, she opened her heart to me. She told me that her need for love was so strong that she just could not seem to get enough love no matter what happened. We both knew where this pattern began in her life, but you cannot go back and change history, and dwelling on it keeps us from claiming our power right now. But still, recognizing that the love around you is not enough can be a very scary feeling. We all know the world is full of people feeling this way. Where do you get more love? How can we fill this never-ending well of hunger for more?

We are all searching for acceptance and belonging in some form from those around us. This is a dangerous place to be because we often will accept it in *any* form and so give power over to others. This need can even manifest in forms of abusive relationships, relationships that just suck the energy from you, or from the gang mentality that young people find so appealing. These relationships are illusions of acceptance or being needed. We receive attention or praise from others and we are elated — for a while. And then we reach for more. We spend our time trying to please others because *maybe* that will bring more of this wonderful feeling. Our ego loves the uplifted feeling it gets from this, basking in this false love and acceptance.

And when this form of love or acceptance is denied or does not show up, we sink into depression or perhaps even frantic actions that result in pushing others away rather than bringing more of that delicious feeling of love. Because we are feeling like there is not enough love, we manifest exactly that — a deficit!

And sometimes as we strive so hard to bring these feelings of love back into our lives so we behave in a way we think will bring approval and acceptance. But the result is we often make promises or speak falsely, saying what we think others want to hear rather than words that reflect our heart's true feelings. Now we fall into a big struggle to match our actions to the false words. When we say that which we *think* others want to hear, we cannot follow through with the actions because it is not what we really need or want, and we end up in a constant struggle both with ourselves and disappointing others.

Letting go of what others think of us, and living authentically from our heart and soul, takes courage, but it then allows us to maintain that beautiful state of feeling loved, accepted and worthy, *regardless* of outside conditions. Tapping into your creative energy source brings that never-ending well of acceptance, love and peace, and as this flows through us and around us, suddenly we begin to attract more loving people to us. We grow in our own self-worth and self-confidence when we begin to see our life changing positively from the work we are doing to strengthen our core and our bond with this powerful well of energy.

Coming to the powerful realization that the conditions around us are not enough is the first step to connecting with your own power. When you recognize that you need and want more, and deserve more, you are able to open to the possibility that there is something more there for you. This is the growing of self, and there is nothing selfish about this at all.

What we *want* is to be selfish. We want love. We want security. We want peace and we want happiness. And we want it all the time, every moment of every day, in abundance. We strive for this because that is what we are made of. That is our natural state. That is what this life force is made of. And we will never be satisfied with finding these feelings from conditions around us. Once we tap into our own *soul power*, we will find it there, in abundance. And once we feel it there in our connection to our creative source energy, then it will follow in manifestations in our life. Belonging, acceptance, security and love first flow from your source, then manifest around you in relationships because you are attracting it to you like a magnet.

As we tap into this source it begins to flow, first as a trickle of water but growing into a stream and then ever-flowing river. And then suddenly people are drawn to you and want to be around you. Things come together in magical ways. Jobs appear, the right people arrive, new friendships form, the perfect mate, the money, the love, the happiness. As we experience our life improving, we cannot forget the steps that brought us here and how it came into our life, or we could fall back into our old ways. Feel the gratitude that you have connected to your higher self and keep doing whatever you need to do to strengthen this bond you have formed.

This feeling will grow stronger and stronger, and suddenly all the *stuff* will not matter anymore as you find you are happier every day. The people around you are energy, and when you are with people that feel your love and centeredness, their energy grows too — rippling out from you it pulls others in, and they are drawn to you like a moth to the flame. There can be an explosion of positive energy between you, *especially* when each person knows that his or her own responsibility is to strengthen their own connection to their higher self.

When we are not seeking from each other, but receiving from our own flow, we become very powerful together. If you stay on this trajectory and do not try to get your energy from others, your relationships become more than you could ever imagine. These become the wonderful relationships you are searching for. And they all begin with you being selfish — selfish enough to do whatever it is you need to do to go within and find your source. It *is* there. We are all connected to this source. If it was not there, you would be dead.

Practice this every day. Your responsibility all day long is to keep checking within — *am I allowing the flow? Or am I searching for it from the outside? Am I looking for approval from others or am I doing what I need to do for me? Are my actions feeling good now and will they feel good tomorrow or in the future too.*

Do what feels good and embrace the things you value most in life. You will begin to follow your heart instincts, and then everything in life will begin to fall into place magically.

Let go of the things that are wasting your time and invest in yourself. Start your day with fifteen to twenty minutes of meditation — see yourself in this flow of energy, take breaks through the day to reconnect, go for walks, spend time alone, take care of yourself by eating food that energizes you, move to music, paint, draw, or write. Take time to do whatever makes you feel closer to your soul every day. You will find the space miraculously opens up in your day allowing you to do this.

Key Notes:
- Slow down to the heartbeat of the earth. Take time to heal and connect to your soul.
- What are your core desires? What is calling to you?
- Take time to be selfish, and stop swimming against the current.
- This is your life — each day is a gift of your life.
- You deserve love, and it is there for you.
- Nothing outside you will give you lasting love, happiness or peace. It all comes from within.

- You will only find your creative soul connection when you slow down to the heartbeat of the earth.
- Check in with your *self* all day long. Are you searching outside or connecting within?
- As you nurture this bond, people will be drawn to you and will want to be around you.

Rhythm of the Earth

There is a rhythm to this earth,
Not man-made at all,
Something natural, pristine,
Existing long before time — but innate to us all;

In the quiet of the morning,
When the sun is just rising,
You can hear the earth's rhythm,
You can feel her heart beat.

Listen — the birds are singing,
Smell the fresh moist grass,
Feel the air, all its newness,
Rainbows glisten in dewdrops.

Time seems to stand still,
Precious moment hanging lightly,
It won't last long — just a breath away,
Onward rhythm keeps pulsing.

Then the sun crests the ridge,
The dew-wet grass dries,
Inviting you to lie down,
Become one with the earth.

As you lie against her breast,
The world awakens around you,
Listen carefully with your soul,
You can feel her heart beat.

Janice Gallant

See yourself through
the eyes of source.

6. Moving Fully into Your Life

Finding Your Power

*"God is said to have looked on all
He created and pronounced it good.
No, He declared it perfect, and so it was.
And since His creations do not change
and last forever, so it is now."*

—A Course in Miracles

Your creative energy source, your life force, is a beautiful and powerful high vibration, which is pure benevolent energy. It is of such a high vibration that it is just not possible for it to even sync with any lower, negative thoughts by you. Your source energy is just not there in the lower vibrations. Source stays in a fresh pristine vibration, regardless of where you are, or what you have done in this life. It sees you as the graceful virtuous soul that is at your core, and it is ever-present for and in you because you *are* creative source energy.

There is nothing you can do that would change this. Because source is such a high vibration, this energy is always drawing you to the higher vibration within you. When you put yourself down or linger in negative thoughts or actions, *you* are moving away from source, but source stays there. It never moves away from you, instead it is always rallying for you to raise your vibration up. You can feel this truth within you. When you wallow in the lower vibrations, you are not very happy. Your days feel heavy and dull and like a lot of hard work. Your goal needs to be always moving towards your higher creative energy that brings with it a sense of fulfillment, peace and joy.

One way to think of your connection is to see it as a beam of light shining down on you. Imagine this light reaches high above you and is connected to a huge vortex in the galaxy. It may help to visualize it like a beautiful, colorful nebula spinning and moving, pulsing with more sheer, sparkling energy and potential than you can ever imagine. Think of the famous Crab Nebula, Cat's Eye Nebula or Helix Nebula. Even though scientists say a nebula is a cloud of dust and gases, they also say it is the place where stars are born. They have immense energy and potential, and that is why I like to visualize my creative energy source as a nebula.

Visualize yourself in this energy — a tiny being floating in this vast sea of energy just soaking up all the pure replenishment you need. You can move away from this light, to the edges of your nebula, but you can never disconnect yourself from it. It is just not possible. You are always connected to this source just like your shadow is always there with you. There are times your shadow appears to dissipate, but it is always there. You can't cut it off or sew it back on like Peter Pan tried to do. It is just there. Your Source streams down to you constantly, never changing, never fading, always there, like an invisible umbilical cord. See yourself as a cocoon of light that gets its energy from this nebula. You are a part of it; it is your life force.

Now sometimes, like our shadows, when we move away from the light source, we fade a bit, only because we place clouds around us blocking the light. But with just our intention, we can move back into the light effortlessly. As you move closer, you can feel the warmth of the light. When we step fully into this source, we can feel not only the warmth but a vibration, a sparkle.

You will feel hope, a lightness in your heart, as you move closer, then excitement, a sense of knowing, enthusiasm, trust, peace, and love. It feels like being in love for the first time. You can feel the fluttering of excitement building and bubbling up inside of you. Think of a time when you have held a newborn baby or a small animal. You held it close to your body and heart and felt that love emanating from them; it cannot help but open your heart just a bit. You can feel your heart softening and expanding. It may have brought tears to your eyes as your heart expanded, and you may have had the feeling of warmth and expansion all around you.

This is what babies bring into this world as they are a pure connection to source, for nothing has happened to cloud their connection to the light. There are no memories or events that have introduced doubt, fear or anger. They are pure connection, and when you hold them, you are feeling this. Their connection is pulling you into alignment with your own source. It is a wonderful feeling that this ripple effect brings to you. This is your return to your creative energy source, feeling it fully opening your heart to the force of love that can flow to you when we allow our connection.

When our beam of light gets faded, it is because we have placed clouds around us. We are not aware of this immense power with which we have lost connection, and life events can cause us to experience feelings of being vulnerable and exposed. We create these clouds as blankets of protection, and we pull them closer imagining this covering will protect us from the harshness of the world around us. We lose trust and feel the loss of our power.

When people lose trust and feel threatened, they move into survival mode and will lash out at those around them. Sometimes we build these blankets into thick walls, imagining that this is where we gain power and control over our lives. These forms of protection are often the result of many diverse events and experiences in life. When experiences in this world are harsh, we lose sight of our true source of power. We are living in the past with fear of the future.

Consider this: if the source has the power to create this world we live in, then you, as a direct extension of this source, most certainly have the power to mold your own life into whatever you want it to be. However, letting these walls down can be very scary, and so there are steps you can take to help you build your trust back up.

The first step is realizing that you are more than this physical body experience you are having. If in fact you are made of this life force energy — and you *are* — then see yourself as a cocoon of light. You will then know that nothing can harm this light. Imagine trying to physically hit the light emanating from a lamp. It is not possible. You are like this light from a lamp only much, much more.

You are a life force light, and nothing can change it, remove it or alter it in any way. It is powerful, and when you allow this light to flow freely, your physical body disappears into the background. You are this source energy having a physical body experience, and when you are finished with your physical body, you will remain as this source energy. And so, nothing here in this world can harm the true you.

The next step involves using I AM statements to power-fully affirm your connection and remove doubts or clouds helping you begin to lower your walls. Blankets of clouds or walls are no protection compared to that of your clear connection with your source. They are illusions of protection. I AM statements recognize your direct-line connection with your source energy, acting like a tuning fork refining your connection. You begin to remember that you can allow this all-powerful source to flow through you and into your life.

Think of your connection with source like a string on a guitar that sometimes gets a little loose. Each time you make a powerful I AM statement, it tightens that string until the vibration is perfect. It pulls you into alignment and strengthens your pathway to your source, like a guitar string that is tuned to perfection, you now have perfect harmony. Your voice is a vibration that can refine your connection to source.

This is why spoken words are powerful. You are either strengthening your connection to source or loosening it up and creating more wobble. You are source energy, and so using statements like I AM powerful, I AM source, I AM love, I AM peace, I AM beauty, I AM expansion, I AM — these pull you into alignment quickly. Nothing is more powerful than your connection with source, but if we are not aware of it, then we are not using our power to the full extension that we are capable of. I AM statements bring your awareness directly to this light again.

Standing fully in your beam of light with your heart open is a powerful and magical experience. Your fears dissipate, and the light shines through, burning up the clouds and crumbling your walls. You are a powerful force just as you are. See yourself standing tall in your light, and feeling stronger, more confident, and self-assured you can easily say and feel, "I AM *that* I AM."

As you begin your day — and *throughout* your day — make I AM statements quietly to yourself to continually remind yourself of your connection to source and the amazing power that you have within you. Whenever you have any doubts throughout your day use I AM statements and your visual image of standing in the direct beam of your higher self. Then trust the guidance and inspiration that comes through to you.

Remember, you are not alone. It is like you have a team of support that is excited to help and support you when you are open to it. The ideas and brilliance in each moment of the day will shine through to you. Answers to problems will come to you. People's behavior around you will change and shift, and suddenly they do not affect you in any negative manner anymore. Their behavior has no effect on who you are standing in the power of your light from source. How can they have any effect on you when you realize your true source? You no longer feel the need to defend yourself in any way, and so their comments or behaviors have no effect on who you are.

You have found a new inner peace and acceptance, a knowing of who you truly are. New doors will begin to open for you as you move to stand more fully in the power of your source. Inspired ideas and synchronicities become a common occurrence in your life, reminding you that you are connected to a powerful universal force. You connect with new people, giving you new experiences and expanding your life in beautiful ways and bringing new opportunities. Your life begins to be filled with abundance in all ways. You are now creating your life with intention.

Key Notes:

- Recognize that you are creative source energy, having a physical experience. It is not something outside of you.
- You are always connected to the powerful life force of creative energy.
- You can move fully into that flow coming from source just by your intention.
- When we place clouds or walls up in an attempt to protect ourselves, our source still remains waiting for us to drop the walls or blow the clouds away.
- Those clouds and walls are illusory protection, the real power is standing fully in your light with an open heart.
- *I AM* statements affirm your connection to source.
- Use *I AM* statements throughout your day to remind yourself and strengthen your relationship with source.
- Watch closely and be aware of results in your life, showing you how being connected to this flow will create positive changes in your life.
- Begin your day with a fifteen to twenty minutes of meditation.
- See yourself through the eyes of source.

Feel gratitude for the struggle,
as it brings clarity of desires,

and then the great heights of exhilaration

when we move back into that
sweet, delicious feeling of alignment

with your creative energy source.

7. The Ebb and Flow

Finding Your Power Again...
and Again... and Again

"Creativity is piercing the mundane to find the marvelous."

—Bill Moyers

Manifesting a life of inspiration and beauty is a daily process. Every day is a new experience. Life is busy, and you will find yourself in and out of the flow. This is completely normal, so do not be too hard on yourself. Expect it and then find the ways to bring yourself back into your creative flow again. With practice and time, you will find it easier and easier to bring yourself back into alignment with your creative energy source.

We all have issues that are occurring and reoccurring in our life. I often find myself catapulted back into the state of fear and helplessness around situations, as I talked about in Chapter 4. Events shift, and suddenly that feeling of trust in the universe has dissipated like a mist. Thoughts keep rolling around in my mind, and I am back living in the past, remembering struggles and deprivation. There are so many of us living out the role of being a victim in our lives, rather than living a life of purposeful creation. We cut ourselves off from our source energy, without realizing what we have done, until the events in our lives manifest in struggles of some kind or another.

Realize that this is the beautiful ebb and flow of life — bringing together contrast, struggle, and then the beauty of breaking through and rising to the clear joy of higher vibration. We can relax into it and enjoy the process. Feel gratitude for the struggle because it brings great heights of exhilaration when we move back into the sweet, delicious feeling of that powerful flow once again.

When I find myself in the storms of life, I must remind myself of the way events in the past have always worked out. Miracles appeared, and so much clarity has come from those difficult times. I know the magic is always there, but sometimes it is hard to see through the rain, and I struggle to grasp a thread and pull it back to me. After all I have learned, I know that it is a feeling I am grasping for, but how do I get there when my mind just keeps pulling up old fears. I recognize that familiar feeling of fear, and I know where I hold it in my body. I am conscious of my need to shift to feelings of peace, happiness, and freedom again, but it seems elusive, and forcing it doesn't work either. The more I struggle, the more elusive it seems to become. This is all about finding my power again.

And so sometimes I wait it out. I breathe. I practice letting go. I trust. Some things in life just need a bit of time. This letting go of control is what can make a shift of light appear through the cracks in the clouds.

There are other times when I struggle to let go. I cannot quite grasp the clarity that is needed, and nothing I do is clearing the clouds. I am aware that it is about having focus and clarity for my manifestations, yet some days I just feel foggy and find my mind continues wandering in circles, going nowhere productive. If I stay here for too long, the stagnation will give way to feelings of frustration and even anger. Believe it or not sometimes this is the place I need to get to, and it often works to pull me out of a slump.

Now this is very important: the trick is not to stay in the frustrated or angry state for long. Use it as a catapult that strengthens and defines your intention and allow it to slingshot you into gratitude and appreciation as quick as possible.

I want to share with you an example of my thought process that has happened in the past. Keep in mind that *creating is a feeling,* and you cannot fake it. You must be feeling it in your heart. This process of venting quite often has occurred in my car, by myself. I am sure I look like a crazy lady, banging on my steering wheel in frustration, venting to the air in front of me. However, the result of it is clarity, lucidity, and a strong desire that rises up into my heart, breaking through the old thought patterns that have clouded my way. My rant can go something like this as I drive down the highway over-thinking the issues in my life:

"I am NOT willing to go back to the victim role that I have played way too often in my life. I will not allow things to happen out of my control or push me around. This is not what I came to this life for. I've had enough scarcity in my life, and I refuse to go back there. This is my life, and I am in control. I AM the manifestor with my creative source — no one else has control over my life. The universe is not punishing me for anything. My source energy is a source of abundance, joy and peace and, therefore, so am I. This is my core life force. And I can change how I perceive all of this right now! I have the power flowing through me that builds worlds and universes! That

same power that is the life force in tiny flowers and huge giant redwood forests is in me too. I choose what happens in my life. I AM the creator, and I want a full expanded life! I want a life full of prosperity in all ways. I want to feel my connection to source every day flowing through me. I want to feel the exhilaration that comes with intentional creation of my life. I want to live life fully, have magical experiences that are shared with my family and friends, I love my family and friends, I love spending time with them, laughing and sharing, I love our family BBQs in our backyard, I love my children and my husband, I love our home and the life we have built, I love my dogs..."

...et cetera, et cetera. And I continue ranting, but now in appreciation and clearly defining what I want for my life.

I can see an image in my mind. It is like I was slipping off the backside of a hill, grasping onto the ice at the top trying to hang on but it is no use, my fingers cannot cling to anything and they keep slipping off. I could feel myself sliding down the hill backwards, panicked, trying to grasp anything. Then suddenly realizing my own power again, I am easily lifted and can feel myself moving back to the top of the hill — first buoyed by anger and determination then by the fullness in my heart, recognizing the power that is there, just waiting for me to open my gates of allowance to this power.

"If I get off this mountain, it's going to be on the front side, where the sun is shining, going forward, laughing and enjoying the whole ride. None of this sliding down backwards, spinning out of control through the shadow side."

I feel taller now and breathe in deeply, feeling the full life force inside me. I can feel that I am a force to be reckoned with now.

I am not standing in that wimpy role anymore. I am the manifestor of my reality. I am in partnership with an immense force available to me anytime. I can feel my heart expanding and growing with these feelings. I picture myself standing on a cliff overlooking the vast ocean. All around me is lush green abundance. I am a magnet drawing in the light of abundance of all forms into my life. It flows through me, swirling all around me in overflow and excess. With this I now feel trust, peace, excitement, freedom and expansion. You cannot have expansion when you are choking on fear. We are here to expand and grow and create. We are here to allow the light and energy to flow, expand, create, and grow.

A flower never stops growing until it dies. We are the same. We are growing every moment, expanding every moment. That is why it feels so awful when we cut off that life force. This life force is your power. Feel this force flowing through your body.

It is important to notice that, through my rant, I went quickly from frustration and anger to my full intentions of what I *did* want and my gratitude for what I have in my life already. I left behind the struggles and did not talk about them, but instead focused on defining what I do want to create in my life. I would shift to one of describing what I want in my life, moving from general description to more detail as my energy lifted in its vibratory level.

It is important to follow the flow of your energy. As my energy lifts, I can feel my heart open and begin to expand, and this is where I feel the gratitude for all I have fill up my heart space. And now, at this point of vibration, I am able to focus and put full intention into creating what I do want in my life. The struggle has brought clarity to my vision.

This is a good place to send my clear thoughts out to the universe. This is a form of prayer and asking for help. I send out my clear intentions to the universe and ask that my intentions match up with that of the universe.

When your desire is very strong, it increases momentum. This is why, when you experience struggles and clarify what you do want, creating with clear intention, things move quickly in the direction that is positive. Coincidences, synchronicities, and inspired ideas happen in this place.

It is so much fun to watch your creations manifest around you in your physical life. When you realize you have guidance and control, you can see life as a fun adventure and not as a continuous struggle. As things get better, your appreciation and trust continues to grow. This is the place you are striving to live from.

Keeping your desire strong can be a challenge when everything is going smoothly in life. Often times, the feeling of contentment settles in. Your desire for change subsides, and you spend time in this place of peace and contentment. There is nothing wrong with this place. It is a good resting place, so you can stay here for a while in this peace and contentment. However, do not forget we are *creators* finding joy in our new inspirations.

If we stay in this comfortable zone too long, be careful that complacency does not seep in also. We can easily drift into our old habits and just float along in life, without much thought about direction. When this happens, our focus and intention may become a bit blurry, and we slip out of the creating with intention mode and live without clear desires for our destiny.

Then something happens, a problem arises, an illness creeps up on us, something happens to jolt our awareness back and this helps to focus our desires once again. Each time you bring yourself back into alignment and focus your intention, you are bringing the potential for miracles and synchronicities back into your life, so it is important to keep a daily practice of your intentions. It is important to keep setting goals and clarifying your strong desires.

The question then becomes this: how do you keep your desire strong even when life is going well? How do you keep momentum going? There is nothing wrong with peace and contentment, but if you have bigger goals in life, you need an intense fuel of desire to reach those goals. How do you keep yourself from feeling bored with your life? How do you keep yourself from falling into those old patterns and slipping back into having those reoccurring problems in your life?

I have given this much thought in my meditations and have come to the realization that this is why our life continues to have that roller coaster effect. I understood that life does have this pattern, but why can't my lows be where my highs are now and my highs become even higher? I want to get the most out of this life in every way possible. I want to keep growing and expanding. How do I keep myself from accepting mediocrity when I feel like life is so amazing now? This is a quote from Wayne Dyer's book *Inspiration* that has had a powerful impact on my understanding about this creating process, and I feel is perfect for this section. I even posted it up on my mirror so I could see it every day.

> *"We need to ask the higher part of ourselves to align with Source, and for the intensity of our desire to be so great that our love for who we are and what we do precludes the possibility of any boredom, tedium, or wariness."*
>
> —Dr. Wayne Dyer, *Inspiration*

And once again the power of the answer comes back to spending time in meditation and focus each morning. Daily practice of meditation will help ease the highs and lows so as you move through life each day you practice creating intentionally And pretty soon, your lows will elevate to be closer to your highs.

The first step each day is connecting with your creative energy source and then reminding yourself what your desires are, visualizing them clearly in your mind. Throughout your day, bring your awareness back to your energy flow, checking in and feeling your heart, finding happiness and appreciation in every moment. And most important, be open to new adventures and opportunities that arise to take your life to new levels.

Key Notes:
- Realize that, as life goes on, you will move in and out of alignment with your creative energy source, and this is normal.
- When going through tough times, hold a candle until you see the light again.
- Remind yourself that things have worked out for you in the past, and they will work out again.
- You can catapult yourself out of a slump by focusing your desires and intentions.
- Strong desire increases momentum, if you keep your intent positive.
- Visualize yourself standing tall on a mountain or hilltop with the creative energy source pouring into you.
- Remember your daily meditation and maintain your daily practice, setting your intention for each day.

- Feel gratitude for the struggle, as it brings clarity of desires, and then the great heights of exhilaration when we move back into that sweet, delicious feeling of alignment with your creative source energy.

My world is magic,

subtle energies are at work here,

creating my reality.

8. Trusting Your Creative Energy Source

Let Go and Allow

"To hold, you must first open your hand. Let go."

—Lao Tzu

We can often feel as though we are on the verge of great things yet at the same time feel like we are just a little stuck. Have you ever wondered, *how do I take a giant leap forward in manifestation? Can the universe please stop playing hide and seek and just tell me how to move beyond this point?* It feels like no matter what you do you are stuck in this one spot in life and cannot move beyond. One thing I do know for sure is that my world is magic, subtle energies are at work here, creating my reality.

There is a power available to us, the immensity of which we, in our little ego-centered lives, cannot fathom. Imagine yourself standing in a field. Now imagine you have a camera focused in on you from directly above your head. You are standing in the field, but you are also viewing yourself through the lens of this camera. Begin to back the camera out, pulling away until you can see yourself standing in this field and you can now also see the edges of this field. Keep pulling away until you see the entire block and all the houses surrounding this field with you standing in the middle of it. As you keep going you may now see the entire town and city. See how much of a tiny speck you are now, fading away as you pull back as high as an airplane.

Your physical body is hardly even perceivable now even though you know it is still there. Keep pulling away until you can see the entire continent below you, then the entire world. Now can you grasp how tiny you are on this incredible earth? It is very humbling, and yet somehow refreshing, to know that you do not require much to survive on this great planet. Now keep pulling away past the moon and the planets, our solar system goes by and we can begin to see the earth in comparison to other planets like Jupiter and Saturn and then of course how tiny our earth is to the great sun.

If you have ever watched one of those videos on the internet that pull you out further, viewing our solar system, and then our entire galaxy on a screen filled with hundreds, no thousands of other galaxies, then maybe, just maybe, you can begin to understand the immensity of source energy. This is all part of the divine source. It pours and moves in and through our universe. We have this energy running through our bodies on a very small scale, but we are able to plug into this power anytime we want.

This source is a pool of pure, high vibrating energy. It is very hard for us to fully grasp, but when you get a glimpse of it, you will understand the power. It is pure, benevolent and beautiful. The closest understanding we have of this energy is the emotion of love. But when I have had moments of connection with this source, the word love

did not even suffice. There was no word for the feeling or
for the immensity of that power. To me it was even greater
than love. It was such a high vibration of light that — even
though this connection was only for a couple of minutes
— I experienced a snippet of the power. I was left with the
clarity that, although our material world is a fun place to
be, nothing here matters at all in the bigger picture.

For all that is important here, our children, family,
friends, all our loved ones, they are there in a higher
dimension in a much bigger form. This world is a mere
shadow of all of us and all there is. However, that being
said, this experience did not diminish my love of our
world or the importance of it for me. In fact, it made my
gratitude for this gift of life even greater and the wonderful
realization that we are here on a great adventure and this is
supposed to be fun! To be here having this physical experience is a true gift, and to be *creating* each day is humbling
and an incredible opportunity.

My focus question was, "how do I manifest desires here
in this world?" And the answer was being shown to me. I
understood instantly that everything here is a much slower
vibratory energy, even the most precious things to us in this
world, no matter how good they are, have a slower vibration. For energy to manifest into material things here on
our world, the vibration needs to slow down. We perceive
our world through our senses. We hear vibration through
our ears, see it through our eyes, smell vibration through
our nose, and of course taste it and feel it through our
touch. In order for us to perceive anything, the energy
needs to first vibrate at a much lower frequency. This high,
pure vibration of source energy is there for us at anytime
anywhere in this world. We do not need to be in a special

location to receive it. It is an ever-flowing fountain of infinite potential. Allowing it to flow into our lives uninhibited is a skill that takes a great deal of practice and persistence to master. It is a craft, a *skill* that you need to develop and fine-tune every day.

This energy is constantly flowing to us. If it was not, we would not exist here in physical form. It is our life force. But we humans have a talent of getting in the way of the pure flow and distorting it into all sorts of problems in our lives.

For example, we begin to manifest something we want — it is taking shape and we can see it coming. In the beginning stages of manifestation, we first feel it move through us with the emotions of joy, love, and exhilaration. These states of mind can help us be in a receiving mode, and this is where inspiration and wonderful new ideas can channel to you. This is the beginning of your manifestations.

Have you ever had a great idea that immediately excited you? You feel energized and get pumped up about it. But you decide to sleep on it and then all sorts of doubts enter your mind. You begin to play over in your mind what your mother, father, siblings, friends and co-workers will say or think about it, or worse yet, you remember similar past experiences and how they turned out, and then that magical energy dissipates.

Or we see it manifesting in our material world and get excited and suddenly 'POOF!' it dissipates and events go sideways. Yup, that is us getting too wrapped up trying to jump into the driver's seat. We tend to interfere with this flow due to our past experiences and problems we may have had along the way. We think we can avoid any possible pitfalls by taking control. I often wonder if we could all just go with the current of our ideas, not get stalled on what others will think, or what has happened in the past, how many more brilliant creations would we have in this world!

Let us back up and slow this down a bit.

This beautiful, infinite potential creative energy courses through us and needs to lower in vibration for us to begin to manifest things into our material world. This is what needs to happen in order for it to manifest in physical form. Our senses can only perceive this pure higher vibration in our physical world when the vibration lowers sufficiently. The vibration must slow down for us to perceive it. When it begins to lower to the vibration of our physical world, we get in the way by trying to control it to fit into our world the way we *think* it should fit. The problem begins when we attempt to manipulate and visualize it into what *we* want, without continually connecting to our higher creative energy source for guidance, thereby redirecting it as the energy lowers.

This pure energy comes to us in the highest purest form without any problems. It comes as pure high vibration, pure benevolent energy ready to create and expand in our world. But as it begins to come through to us, what we think about it and how we feel *shifts* this energy. When we bring it through, we see it, hear it, or feel it as a problem because this has been the recurring past experiences in our lives.

We are the ones getting in the way of this pure form, with doubts, reliving past problems and dwelling on all the issues that have brought us heartbreak and heartache. We interfere by imposing our own expectation of what this vibration should look like, or feel like without even realizing we are doing it. This is why staying in the moment — not in the past or worrying about the future — is so important. Stay in the moment connected to your creative energy source. Do not try to manipulate the manifestation no matter how much you want it to be the outcome of your choice. Trust that your creative energy source can handle it — and handle it even better than you could ever have imagined.

Moving into a higher vibration than what you are used to can sometimes be a bit of an up-and-down process. New experiences are new energy, and sometimes this raises the alarms in our ego. If it is outside of our past experiences — meaning we have not experienced this before and are not sure where it should fit — we often shift it around until it fits into something familiar to us, like an old pattern. Even if it is something we have been dreaming about or a goal we have been trying to reach.

When it is brand new energy of a higher vibration, we may unconsciously sabotage ourselves because the unfamiliar is not as comfortable for us as old energy. We know we can handle the old energy patterns as we have done it in the past. We repeat these patterns in our life. We think the same thoughts and follow the same mental thought patterns. The unconscious thoughts are there, and until we take the time and commit to making changes in the way we think, life will keep giving us the same thing, over and over again. Nothing happens by accident. We are all creators, creating our lives, day by day.

> *It is the thoughts <u>between</u> your conscious thoughts that create your world.*

To move into the new higher vibration requires courage to shift our daily world and our thought patterns. Your creative energy source is bringing things to you at a pace to help prepare you for the new and improved life you are wanting. Trusting and allowing will help bring everything to you at exactly the right time.

We need to go to the source and perceive it at its purest form, its highest vibration, and hold that pure form as it manifests into reality. Allow it to flow in its most beautiful, pristine form — just flowing through you like magic! You need to match up to the higher desires of source, and you do that by connecting to your source and working on nurturing that connection until it is with you all day. When you allow this energy to flow and create with freedom, your life will be filled with beauty and magic, manifesting your desires in ways you never thought of. As you learn to raise your frequency up to the higher vibration of source, you will be more in harmony with your desires. Your desires need to match up with the desires of the source.

Now this does not mean that you cannot have that new car, or house, job or the perfect health you want. Your creative energy source is all about creating here on earth and enjoying all the pleasures of this earth. However, if your desires are ego-based, then you may find that you will eventually move away from them, as they will not be as important to you anymore, and the manifesting power diminishes.

This is a good spot to include some thoughts on spiritual abundance versus material abundance. You will find that the first step to mastering the craft of *manifesting* is to be a manifestor of spiritual abundance. This means you will easily manifest feelings of peace, love, and happiness into your life at a moment's notice, and your life will reflect an abundance of this. Feeling happiness and swells of love when you are with your family and friends will give you more and more appreciation for your life, and feelings of gratitude will roll through your days more and more often.

When you are in this space you will find it easier to manifest the material objects or experiences that you want in your life. It is from this vantage point that you can manifest your material desires. What you may find is that material objects will not matter as much anymore. Your heart will be so filled up that you may re-evaluate your original desires. There is nothing wrong with this. You are learning to live from your heart and not your ego. There is also nothing wrong with wanting more material abundance.

We live in a physical world, and we are here to enjoy these experiences. Creating beautiful spaces, objects, and visiting beautiful places are intrinsic to us as creators. But what happens when we reach this point of manifesting is that we begin to create in a more responsible way. When we are connected to our energy source, we are following inspiration and guidance from a much higher perspective. As you fill your life with material objects that you have desired, you will now be taking on the responsibility and desire to help others reach this space also. You will be pulling them up to where you are, helping them find a life of spiritual abundance and then their own material manifestations.

I believe that moving through these stages of spiritual growth slowly and allowing yourself to grow into a more balanced, responsible caretaker of your world is very important. You will find, as you shift your desires, you will manifest objects for different purposes. And this will expand your energy even more.

Wealthy people have a responsibility to hold the space for everyone so they may in turn reach higher and evolve in their lives. Wealthy, abundant people are some of the best visionaries of our world. They help catapult us forward on the edge of continuous creation, by giving us the resources to solve the problems of the world and inspire us as *creators*. Philanthropy combined with spiritual awareness reaches out to everyone, creating a ripple effect in our world and inspires everyone to expand their own energy and bring in more happiness and peace. This is not about going out and pushing your beliefs on anyone. It is about quietly living a life of freedom from ego and having full abundance in every way, with a strong connection to your higher self, allowing inspiration to guide you.

This is true freedom.

If you think about it, everything you desire, you desire to give you more freedom; freedom from bonds, freedom to create, freedom to do what you want to do, freedom to be yourself, etc. We desire freedom in everything we want. We crave freedom because this is the core of who we are. The life force that is flowing through our body is this pure, high vibration of creative energy that is love and freedom. Love brings complete acceptance. Freedom brings creativity, growth, and expansion. If we allow this pure energy to flow through us and have the freedom to create, we can't even begin to imagine what that freedom will bring to our lives! This is co-creating with source at its best! This is what is meant by *let go and allow*.

So how do we allow this beautiful, pure energy to flow into our world and keep our thoughts out of the way of its wonderful creations?

You have already projected your dreams and desires out to the universe, now let go of the steering wheel and just let your creative energy source create. Trust in this vast, endless source. When you tap into this source, you begin to feel the power that is there for you. This energy flows through your heart into your world, so it makes sense that your heart needs to be filled with joy and appreciation for your life. When the negative emotions — like doubt, anger resentment or frustration — come in they block the flow from manifesting in the positive, magnificent ways it can create.

You need to find ways to be happy and light in the moment. This is why, at the beginning of this book, I talked about making space for you. You need to be finding happiness for yourself first. As you do this and your world shifts to creating beautiful experiences, this will have a ripple effect outward to everyone around you. Your heart must remain open for this pure energy to flow freely. Stay connected through your daily meditation, trusting and allowing the flow to move through you. Whenever you feel yourself gripping the steering wheel, step back, take a deep breath, and trust in the process. There are bigger forces at work here. Be grateful for this help, send your thoughts of gratitude out to the world, expand your heart and just let go.

When you recognize the endless stream of power that is flowing to you, with the infinite potential to create anything you want in your life, and you *feel* this power, then nothing else matters. When you are basking in this feeling of pure love, you no longer need to find it in anyone else or anything. Your biggest desire becomes wanting to stay in this beautiful connection forever because it *feels* so delicious!

Key Notes:
- Recognize that you are a speck in this vast universe and you draw very little from the pool of your creative energy source to manifest a life of your dreams.
- This pure, high energy source needs to slow its vibration down to materialize in our world.
- As things begin to manifest for you, stay connected to your creative energy source, trusting and allowing this manifestation to present itself in the best way for your own growth. Try not to manipulate it.
- Let go of the steering wheel.
- Be open to new energy and experiences in your life.
- Recognize spiritual abundance is the first step to material abundance. You are on the right path!

One

We are gifted upon a path,
each in a journey entwined.
Amongst the forest dense
some ways are hard to find.

Each journey's alone it seems,
but let your awareness heighten.
There in the midst of the forest,
your guides await to enlighten.

Clear eyes will find upon your path,
that you are not alone,
but connected to the forest,
when traveling to find your home.

Each pebble points the way,
peaceful cedars inscribe the teachings,
and whispering leaves reveal the secrets.
In silence the way is clearing.

So lift your eyes from downward gaze,
flow with the spirit seas.
In the forest that seems entwined,
guides dance lightly with the trees.

And there amid tangled roots,
where rocks and branches lay,
your path will lighten,
as your gaze stays focused.

On the Star of One that guides your way.

Janice Gallant

Conclusion: Why I Am Never Satisfied?

Why I Am Always Seeking!

"You can't use up creativity.
The more you use, the more you have."

—Maya Angelou

"Why are you never happy?"

This question — from the introductory chapter — was one I often heard in my head, posed in the voices of people from my past. You see, as someone who was constantly seeking, it appeared to others like I was not content with my life. I needed to be learning, growing, and experiencing the next new thing, and that made others a bit uncomfortable. But that is okay because I was okay with my movement in life. I simply am a creator, a seeker, and I was constantly recreating my life.

Whenever things settled and became too routine, I needed to move on to something new. I did this recreating through my work and my hobbies and — to the chagrin of my husband — in the early years I wanted to change houses too. So the answer to this question is really quite simple, and I hope that, by the time you reach this point in the book, you will also feel this barely needs addressing. However, since I began this book with this question, I did promise to conclude with it at the end.

It has been a question I have heard directed towards me in years past. It used to bother me and make me feel inadequate as if there were something wrong with me. But it was never a question of my happiness. I was always very happy; I just wanted to create more. These voices made me feel guilty about this seeking — as though to suggest that I should be happy to be content and stay right there. My restlessness was intrinsic and *not* something I could control because at the core of all of us is a creator energy. I have come to treasure and commune with this wonderful part of my being.

Constant movement is unavoidable in our lives. Our bodies are always moving, growing, expanding. Cells are dividing, breath is moving in and out. Our minds are always moving forward, creating. Our beautiful earth and solar system are the same way. Constantly moving, pulsing, and cycling. Life cycles, water cycles, carbon cycles, rock cycles all renewing, recreating and rebuilding.

What is it that tells our cells to divide? Particles do not create more particles; there is something else involved and *it* is our life force — our creative energy source. This creative life force tells the seed to grow as it absorbs the nutrients required to accomplish this. It flows in the seeds of grass, plants, trees, birds and animals, and it flows through us too. We are filled with this same life force energy moving through us in every breath we take. Why do you breathe? What is the force that causes your lungs to breathe in, expand and release, only to do it again in the next moment? It requires no conscious thought because life force energy keeps our breath moving in and out and our heart beating and beating and beating.

It is not a great leap, then, if everything in this world is flowing, moving, growing, expanding, to understand how natural it is for our minds and souls to have the continual urge to do the same. We are creative energy, and it is not possible for us to sit stagnantly. Our life force is the one that creates worlds, creates beautiful landscapes, sunrises and sunsets. We were born to create.

We have created this world. Look how far we have come and all the creativity that was required to get where we are. Look around you at the roads, the houses, the buildings, all the magnificent, creative inspiration required to clear the space, create the designs and then implement the action to build the city around you. We are creators, creating a world that brings ease for everyone, beauty and aesthetics in design with the environment around us. We are learning and growing from our ancestor's creations and from our own past actions. But we keep moving forward because this is what we are made of — creative energy!

If you are creating through your work, your love, your passion, your mind, your body, then you are doing what you came here to do. You are happiest when things are moving forward in an inspiring way. Think of that exhilaration you feel when a new idea comes to you. It brings with it fresh energy along with hope of a brighter future.

When things slow down in our lives without any change, stagnation slowly settles in, and we become restless, bored, uninspired, and at times downright cranky. As events in our lives become challenging, we are pushed further to grow and expand in new ways. This may be painful in the process, but the elation we feel when we come through it cannot be replaced with any other feeling. We are newly expanded beings and can never go back to the person we were before. However, we can gain control of our creating so that these challenges are fun and exciting instead of fearful and stressful. This is our goal as we move fully into our creative energy source.

Learn to be open to and embrace changes,
new careers, new relationships, new
experiences as you follow your heart and
your inspirations. This will lead you to a life
of excitement, fulfillment, inner peace and
happiness. This will manifest your dreams.

May you have many blessed
creations my friends!

*"Once you make a decision,
the Universe conspires to make it happen."*

—Ralph Waldo Emerson

APPENDIX

Meditation Process — Getting Ready

You do not need to do anything to get ready for mediation. However, through the years, I have found a few things that have become a bit of a ritual for me and have helped me incorporate my meditation practice into something more regular. I try to meditate every day and ideally twice a day — but let's face it, we are all human and life does get demanding sometimes.

Do not be hard on yourself if you miss your practice or go for a week at a time without meditating. You will soon find that it becomes more and more important to you, and you will begin to not let other things get in the way of your special quiet time. The dishes will be there later. Sit down and give yourself a few minutes. Here are some suggestions, none of these are required and are not rules. It is important to just follow what feels most comfortable for you:

Create a special space that will be your meditation spot — this could be a corner of your bedroom, a special chair in your living room, or even just the kitchen table. It is nice to have it always set up as this saves you time and you will be more apt to sit and meditate more frequently. If you use a chair, be sure to be able to sit up straight and have your feet on the floor. Or you could sit on the floor on a cushion. Having a straight back allows energy to flow smoothly. However, when I began I just sat on my sofa.

- If possible, try to be facing east.
- Light a white candle.
- Put some special objects around your candle that bring peaceful thoughts to your mind. These could be crystals, rosary beads or a cross, a Buddha figure, anything that you relate to as signs of peace and higher vibrations.
- Having soft meditative music, or nature sounds in the background helps. Especially if you have pets. These will block out other noises and your pets will begin to know that this is quiet time and will lay down to sleep near you.
- If you can meditate at the same time each day this is good. Set aside ten to fifteen minutes to begin with and slowly allow for more time as you can. I find that fifteen minutes every day can be more powerful than thirty minutes twice a week. However, any time you can meditate is very beneficial.
- You may want to hold a special object in the palm of your hands (a crystal, rosary beads, cross, etc.).

Meditation — Grounding and Centering

Read through this mediation and then close your eyes and follow the directions:

Get comfortable and breathe deeply. Inhale through your nose right down into your belly, and relax as you let the air go through your mouth. Do this three more times, focusing on relaxing as you breathe out.

Now breathe normally, and as you breathe in, imagine a crystal clear pure white light filling you up. As you breathe out, imagine all the negative energy and stress releasing from your body and flowing out easily and effortlessly. Breathe in pure white light flowing into all areas of your body, releasing any negative energy or stress.

See the white light gently filling and flowing through your body, arms, and legs right down into your toes. It glows and fills every fibre and cell in your body and around your body. See it filling your head, through all areas of your brain, down your spine, your legs and expanding to fill all your organs and tissues. This white light moves and flows easily through your body, cleansing and relaxing all areas.

Now imagine this light flowing down through your feet into the floor. It flows down easily like roots into the earth, into the soil, flowing down easily like it is a river flowing down into the earth, past all the rocks searching for the center of the beautiful, magnificent crystalline center of our earth. And there it is rejuvenated and magnified with the pure energy of the earth, cycling back up, following the path back up to your feet. Flowing up through your feet, up your calves, your thighs, past your hips, flowing through your abdomen, following your core up through your head and out the top of your head.

This beautiful pure energized light flows upward connecting your core to a sparkling star over your head. This star is connected to the universal energy, follow this flow up as it pours upward to the vast universe to the light, the divine light, your nebula or vortex of creative energy source. The light grows and strengthens, communing with this energy and continues to flow back down to you through your star, in through the top of your head, down through your body, your legs, your feet and back down to the center of the earth.

This cycle continues from the earth through your body, out the top of your head, through your star to the universal energy and back down again. Each time, the core of light flowing through your body expands and strengthens, filling you with pure light, leaving no room for any negative energy or stress in any part of your body. Flowing and cleansing it continues, and you feel more and more at peace, finding the rhythm of the universe, along with the heartbeat of the earth.

Your light now expands and not only fills your body but *surrounds* your body like a cocoon of light. Allow this energy to continue to flow until you feel revived, balanced and energized.

When you feel you are ready begin your day, stretch, and wiggle your fingers and toes, bringing yourself back to your space with a sense of peace that will follow you throughout the day. As your day unfolds, try to take a minute a few times throughout the day to visualize yourself in this cocoon of light connected to the earth and your nebula. Breathe deeply. Release.

Acknowledgements and Gratitude

We receive understanding through the sharing of our experiences and through good teaching. Through these avenues, we can help each other come to new understandings and a more attuned awareness. As we learn we absorb the new information, we feel out the truth as it resonates through us. We begin to use these newly formed beliefs to guide us day to day. The results coming from this fresh information materializes around us in our daily life. And if you are a student of self-awareness and manifesting, you are always observing the material world around you, reflecting and juxtaposing these events with your own thoughts and feelings.

I have always known there was something more to our world than what meets the eye. Even as a small child, I was spiritually seeking. This has been a passion for me for as long as I can remember, and I have spent many years reading, learning, meditating and reflecting in order to grow my self-awareness. I want to express my gratitude and appreciation to those who have been the brave ones, the teachers who pioneered and brought this information forward from *spirit*. The teachings from these authors in particular have been a guiding light in my life and helped me through many challenges. My heart is full of gratitude for the written work of:

Abraham, through Esther & Jerry Hicks
A Course in Miracles, brought forward through
Helen Schucman & William Thetford
Dr. Wayne Dyer

Their work has helped create depth and understanding, and along with my own visions and experiences, I have come to a level of *knowing*. I can't express the level of gratitude I have for their guidance through their written work.

As much as we can understand the teaching and feel the truth, *knowing* comes from personal experience. My words in this book are mine, and come from over thirty-five years of learning, reflecting, and continuous questioning that was solidified through my personal visions and epiphanies. So many times, I would receive clarity in a vision during meditation, bringing my understanding to a new level of *knowing*. Meditation has been foundational to my own knowing.

Spirit reaches out to all of us. The information available to us is universal. There is nothing new to say (right now), but by sharing our experiences through words, perhaps we can each reach our own epiphanies that bring *knowing* to all of us who seek it.

Furthermore, I would like to sincerely thank those who have encouraged me to take this journey to its fullest form:

To my dear friend Melba Amos who has been with me since the beginning of my spiritual quest; her own authentic journey has inspired me many, many times. Thank you for all the cups of coffee, garden walks, and long-distance phone conversations!

To my sisters, Sue and Alisa, and my brother, Pete, who have shared my journey since the beginning. We have helped each other become better, stronger people in so many various ways. I would not have wanted to be on this journey without you joining along on this ride of life. To my mother, Gale, who gave me my strength and the confidence to live my life to the fullest and to my father, Ross, who introduced the world of art and gentleness to my life.

To my first readers: Chandel, Sue, Pete, Melba, Karilynn, Paulette, Rhonda, Char, Jan, Carol, and Jean for all your kind words of support, advice, and encouragement. To Carol for blazing the trail with her book, *Smiling Single Mom*, showing me that becoming a published writer can be done! To Jean for her brilliant proofreading and editing! To Katherine for Moon Star Lodge teachings that enhanced my development through her sacred circle, which created the space for my foundational learning. And finally, to my community of Olds for all the support and encouragement I have received for all my creative work as an artist! The enthusiasm for the arts in this community continues to inspire me!

For more information about
Janice Gallant Art & Writing

Visit:

www.janicegallant.com
or
www.thecreationguild.com

For further information on Rubenfeld Synergy contact:
Melba Amos, Certified Rubenfeld Synergist, Changes Now
https://www.facebook.com/CRSchangesnow/

CPSIA information can be obtained
at www.ICGtesting.com
Printed in the USA
FSHW01n0111211018
53155FS